CHANGE FORCES IN POST-COMMUNIST EASTERN EUROPE

This book seeks to illuminate some important features of the forces that shape sudden and dramatic large-scale educational reform. It also suggests new directions in the study of educational change with the potential to guide strategic planning of the transformation of education in societies where change is profound and rapid. It does so by exploring recent educational changes in five post-Soviet nations: Russia, the Czech Republic, Romania, Hungary, and East Germany, against a conceptual framework developed by Fullan (2001) for understanding large-scale educational reform.

The book itself is organized into three parts. In Part I, Michael Fullan introduces the dynamic forces of large-scale reform and explores issues related to reform in countries experiencing sudden and dramatic transformation. He begins with a discussion of the "Triple I" model that encompasses three broad phases of change: initiation, implementation, and institutionalization. He then addresses three additional themes that strengthen the applicability of the Triple I model: the "coherence-making problem" of multiple innovations, characteristic of large-scale reform; the importance of applying simultaneous pressure and support to sustain change; and the creation of new infrastructure capacities to facilitate successful change.

In Part II, each of the five chapters presents a case study of a different country. Each contributor examines the dynamic process of change over time, identifying salient themes, delineating critical factors, and examining their consequences and impact on their education system. "The value of case studies [within comparative education]," as Arnove (2001) points out, "resides in their contribution to the refinement and modification of extant theory and ultimately to the creation of new theory when existing explanatory frameworks are not applicable" (p. 496).

In Part III, Fullan reflects on the insights provided by the authors in Part II, and proposes a new emergent conceptual framework for guiding the thinking and strategic planning of transformation of education in large-scale reform.

CHANGE FORCES IN POST-COMMUNIST EASTERN EUROPE

Education in transition

Edited by
Eleoussa Polyzoi

Michael Fullan

John P. Anchan

RoutledgeFalmer
Taylor & Francis Group

LONDON AND NEW YORK

First published 2003
by RoutledgeFalmer
11 New Fetter Lane, London EC4P 4EE

Simultaneously published in the USA and Canada
by Routledge
29 West 35th Street, New York, NY 10001

RoutledgeFalmer is an imprint of the Taylor & Francis Group

© 2003 Eleoussa Polyzoi

Typeset in Goudy by Sparks Computer Solutions, Oxford
Printed and bound in Great Britain by
MPG Books Ltd, Bodmin

British Library Cataloguing in Publication Data
A catalogue record for this book is available from the British Library

Library of Congress Cataloging in Publication Data
Change forces in post-communist Eastern Europe : education in
transition / [edited by]
Eleoussa Polyzoi, Michael Fullan, and John P. Anchan.
p. cm.
Includes bibliographical references and index.
1. Educational change–Europe, Central–Cross-cultural studies.
2. Educational planning–Europe, Central–Cross-cultural studies.
3. Post-communism–Europe, Central–Cross-cultural studies. I. Polyzoi,
Eleoussa. II. Fullan, Michael. III. Anchan, John P.
LA622.7.C53 2003
370'.947–dc21
2003041391

ISBN 0 415 30659 0

To Dimos, Ian, Panayiotis, Konstantine
Zynu, Sneha, Krupa, and
our Eastern European colleagues

CONTENTS

ILLUSTRATIONS AND TABLES

Figures

Tables

CONTRIBUTORS

John P. Anchan teaches at the University of Winnipeg, Manitoba, Canada. Besides teaching at the University of Alberta, he has served as Executive Director of Edmonton Immigrant Services Association (EISA), a non-profit charitable settlement organization. John has taught in India, United Arab Emirates, and Canada, and has published in his areas of interest including development education, information technology, culture and education, global education, and contemporary sociological issues in education.

Nina Arnhold holds a Ph.D. in Comparative and International Education from the University of Oxford. She has worked as a consultant for UNESCO and for the Boston Consulting Group. As a project leader at the Centre for Higher Education Development, she is currently involved in the reform of higher education institutions in Germany. Her research interests include higher education, teacher education, education for reconstruction, and education in countries in transition.

Cesar Bîrzea is Director of the Institute of Education Sciences in Bucharest (a National Institute of Research and Development in Education, supported by the Ministry of Education) and Professor at the University of Bucharest. He has also served as President of the National Council on Educational Reform in Romania, member of the Education Committee of the Council of Europe (Strasbourg), and President of the IBE Council (Geneva). His research interests include educational policies in transition countries, educational change, education for democratic citizenship, and global education.

Marie Černá is Head of the Department of Special Education, Charles University, Prague, the Czech Republic. She has held various academic and administrative posts at the university, including Vice-Dean of International Relations. She has published numerous scholarly papers on educational reform, special education, and educational policy. Her current research focuses on the quality of life of mentally challenged adults.

Eduard Dneprov is the former Minister of Education of the Russian Federation who ushered in major reform in the early 1990s. He is former director of the Federal Institute for Educational Planning, Ministry of Education of the Russian Federation. Currently, he is Professor of History, University of the Russian Academy of Education. He has published widely on the history of education, policy, and reform in the Russian Federation.

Ciprian Fartușnic is a Senior Researcher with the Romanian Institute of Education Sciences (Educational System Evaluation Department) and the Romanian National Observatory. He is also a teaching assistant and consultant on educational issues for the Romanian Academic Society. His main research interests include management and financing in education, rural and intercultural education, civil society involvement in educational policies, and vocational education and training.

Michael Fullan is Dean of the Ontario Institute for Studies in Education at the University of Toronto. An innovator and international leader in teacher education, he has published widely on the topic of educational change. He has received numerous awards, including the Canadian Education Association 'Whitworth Award for Educational Research' in June 1997.

Gábor Halász is Director-General of the National Institute of Public Education in Budapest. He also teaches education at the University of Miskolc. His research fields are education policy and administration, comparative and international education, and theory of education systems. He has worked as an expert consultant for a number of international organizations, particularly OECD, the World Bank, and the Council of Europe. As an education policy expert, he took an active part in Hungary's educational-change process in the 1990s.

Eleoussa Polyzoi is Professor of Education and Coordinator of Developmental Studies at The University of Winnipeg, Manitoba, Canada. She has published widely in the areas of language development, childcare, school evaluation, and comparative education. Her research interests include educational change theory and practice, particularly as they relate to post-Soviet countries.

FOREWORD

Change – as the common cliché goes – is the only constant. This paradoxical statement aptly describes the continuous evolution of contemporary society, influenced as it is by information technologies and reeling from the effects of globalization. As a result, those engaged in the attempt to understand organizational change may find the exercise somewhat traumatic. While change at the personal level may be discomfiting, systemic structural change tends to be far more complex and far less amenable to analysis, let alone to a planned response. In a world characterized by a proliferation of theoretical constructs and political persuasions, change has been explored within the context of multifarious theories, including modernization, neo-Marxism, liberalism, liberationalism (empowerment, critical pedagogy), post-colonialism, and postmodernism, to name just a few. Beyond the traditional theories, we also have business models of change, as well as models of social change, jurisprudence and change, pedagogical change, and change in relation to capitalist and conditioned states (Sieber, 1972; Carnoy, 1974; Carnoy and Samoff, 1990; Zakharieva, 1991; Hodgkinson, 1991; McLeish, 1996; Carter, 1997). More recently, researchers have analysed the challenge of change during transition in the Baltic States during the 1990s (Peck and Mays, 2000). In essence, the Baltic initiative confirmed that educators and policymakers in the ex-Soviet blocs (Lithuania, Estonia, and Latvia) have faced innumerable challenges in the process of re-inventing and redefining the policy of educational change. The Baltic case studies also re-affirm our stance that *change* can be not only complex but also difficult to analyse. The elimination of an historical and obsolete infrastructure followed by the replacement of a new educational system involves a drastic restructuring that decentralizes state-controlled apparatuses that would have essentially served as ideological employ of the erstwhile powers. As elucidated by Mays (2000), devolution of powers and re-building (what Bîrzea would explain as 'rectification') are usually accompanied by uncertainty as reformers are forced to deal with a population plagued with unrest and apprehension (p. 193).

Despite the wide range of theoretical explanations, a clear understanding of the role and influence of education within this complex world of change remains elusive to many policy- and decision-makers. Educational systems are diverse in nature, a reflection of diverse cultures, peoples, and histories; consequently, the assumption that the field of international and comparative education can provide us with easy and tangible solutions may be naïve and even misleading. The claim has been made that, historically, theories of modernization, initiatives like the green revolution, and the development policies of international institutions (e.g. International Monetary Fund, World Bank, United Nations Development Program, World Trade Organization, Organization for Economic Cooperation and Development) have largely resulted in convoluted policies, disrupted development, and incessant turmoil – particularly in developing nations (Eisenstadt, 1974; Toh, 1980; Hurst, 1981; Larrain, 1983, 1989, 1994, 2000; Zakharieva, 1991; Arnold, 1994; Carlsson and Ramphal, 1995; Mason, 1997). Nevertheless, despite all its associated difficulties, change neither can nor should be avoided. Hence, researchers continue their investigations, in the hope of better understanding a complex world that is continually in the process of change. In particular, historically, the contribution of comparative and/or international education – as a specialized field of academic discourse – has provided invaluable insights into understanding global changes (Torres, 2001; Arnove, 2001).

While many political economists and development theorists have attempted to explicate the concept of change (especially in relation to developing countries), educational change, for the most part, has been analysed as an event rather than as a process. Fullan's approach attempts to address this limitation. Political scientists and development theorists have variously formulated the process of change as *growth* (Spencer, Durkheim, Robertson), *transition* (Carnoy and Samoff, 1990), *transformation* (Freire, 1978, 1983, 1985; Allahar, 1989), *development* (Bernstein), *evolution* (Spencer), and *modernization/industrialization* (Parsons). For some, 'change' refers to developing from *simple* to *complex* (Comte, Weber); for others (structural functionalists), change involves a response to tensions between the superstructure and the economic base. The plethora of explanations has generated a great deal of theoretical discourse, which has remained largely pedantic, yielding little in the way of practical insight (Shapiro, 1998). The brilliant analytical treatises of economic determinism have not delivered practical solutions for educators looking for answers. Descriptive accounts of the causes of change abound; what is lacking are 'models' which could serve as precursors to further development of explanatory frameworks. Although Beeby's sincere but unsuccessful attempt to provide an evolutionary model (1967, 1969) did draw some attention to the concept of directed planning (Guthrie, 1980), educational change has largely been explored in terms of socio-political change. Some writers have attempted to redress this limitation; Fullan's work in the past 15 years, for example, has directed attention to the understanding of planned educational change – albeit, not within the context of comparative or development education. Fullan's analysis, which provides insights into change at the micro-level of school and classroom, may, to a certain degree, be applicable to the macro-level of comparative and international education. Within this context, Fullan's model may not only offer some insight into change as a process but also facilitate the analysis of change within the current geopolitical context. One cannot use simplistic measures to assess educational change, nor conduct social analysis in isolation from the various political, social, and historical influences that have an impact upon it. Fullan's ideas, applied to exploratory research, may allow us to re-examine experiences and case studies in order to engage our theoretical under-standings and underlying assumptions of *change*, and to use this understanding as the backdrop for our investigation of case studies.

Post-Communist Eastern Europe offers us an opportunity to consider countries that have gone through revolutionary, rather than the more familiar evolution-ary, changes. As Bîrzea (1994) argues, transition may be defined or understood in various ways, and yet it defies a universal explanation; Arnhold, in Part II of this book, takes this stance in her attempt to explain the changes which oc-curred after the reunification of Germany. If political and economic changes defy successful analysis, how much more so do cultural transitions? Arnhold describes the attempt made by Oxford educators to link education and transi-tion. An important feature of their model is the recognition that change cannot be understood as linear or sequential. Although the model's proposed phases suggest a sequence, this could be understood in terms of processes rather than events. The complexity of educational change is evident in what Fullan (2001, p. 52) describes as 'operations across ... many levels'. The East German case study furnishes an excellent illustration of this complexity: in this example, a power shift from teachers to parents is observed. As teachers traversed successive stages of change – from initial euphoria, through struggles with sudden, drastic, and uncontrollable upheaval, to loss of power and resultant confusion – they suffered stress and bore the brunt of public consternation. Nevertheless, these teachers recognized that change – uncomfortable as it may be – may help them to become critical educators. They also realized the value of historical analyses in under-standing some of the tensions experienced during change. It could be said that democracy offers the freedom to become uncomfortable with the unknown, to move from the known to the unknown in pursuit of something better. In spite of its weaknesses and ambiguities, the freedom to experiment bestows the reality of empowerment. Indeed, democratic process may be subverted by individuals, who arrogate decision-making power to themselves. Tharoor (1997) in his musings *India: From Midnight to the Millennium* puts this into perspective: 'Yes, democracy can be unbearably inefficient but efficiency without democracy can be simply unbearable' (p. 360).

Using Fullan's model as the framework for analysis, Halász investigates educational/social change in post-Communist Hungary; Bîrzea and Fartuşnic consider the intricacies of change in Romania; and Polyzoi and Dneprov ap-praise Russia, a nation which has struggled to extricate itself from powerful and contradictory political and economic forces within an overwhelmingly capitalist world order. All these studies strive to realize a better understanding of structural and systemic change using Fullan's proposition; the authors make no incredible claims to explain all the inexplicable changes, and rightly so. Rather, they offer an examination of the unique historical changes that have occurred in seemingly disparate national entities which nonetheless share certain commonalities – an investigation that may perhaps enable educational analysts to further explore the phenomenon of change per se.

As most theories are subject to contextual, particularistic, and historical influences, the attempt to generalize can be detrimental to any scholarly pursuit. Likewise, the attempt to supply grandiose, universal metanarratives would be a futile and inappropriate task. Nevertheless – whether in Halász's attempt to analyse educational/social change in post-Communist Hungary, in Bîrzea and Fartușnic's examination of change in Romania, or, especially, in the Russian case study contributed by Polyzoi and Dneprov – the challenging exercise of exploring the appropriateness of one or more theoretical explanations in relation to other contexts may lead us to hitherto unforeseeable answers. Research is not only a planned rendezvous with knowledge; it is also a rewarding activity which may include serendipitous elements. It may be helpful to remind ourselves that change is not a new concept or phenomenon; it is our evolving notions of change in relation to our world which make this study an interesting and relevant polemic exercise – a humble attempt to explicate the complexities of change itself.

As a complex process involving the interaction of multiple variables (including units of analysis, the nation's history, politics, economics, and many others), the task of understanding change is by no means simple. But, another (more profound and subtle) reason exists for the difficulty: our understanding is conditioned inescapably by our own subjectivity. One of the strengths of this book is that it embodies this insight. Rather than claim expertise and theorize from without, seeking to explain the *Other*, it presents the experiential *and* researched analyses of intellectuals living their lives within the changes being explicated. These are the voices of those who are part of the change, individuals who not only have played vital roles in policy development in their countries but who also engage in meaningful and formal analyses, from their own perspectives, of how transition has occurred. From a post-modern and especially from a post-colonial standpoint, the voices of these subjects demonstrate increasing movement towards the centre – from the marginal to the essential, from the peripheral to the core. These voices constitute their own authority; they need no authentication from 'experts' elsewhere. They narrate their own stories in their own language. Most of the contributors have played important roles in the changes they describe; because of this, some may question the 'objectivity' of their perceptions/understanding – this is ironic, considering that we at the centre have admitted no need to validate our knowledge of the periphery or of the narrator's lived experiences (it is not surprising that action research has gained such popularity in recent times). While these writers share to some extent a common political past, they represent very diverse nations: their divergent experiences enrich this collection. As always, in the field of comparative education (which some may prefer to call *international education*), we must continue to grapple with the tensions inherent in analysis of processes taking place in disparate situations. We have sought to infuse greater clarity into the discourse by use of Fullan's conceptual framework for understanding transition. Our discussion does not purport to provide irrefragable answers; it deals, rather, with the possibility of initiating meaningful inquiry into the process we call *change* – a phenomenon that defies unproblematic explanation.

Perhaps it is also important to remind our readers that this book positions itself within the domain of education, rather than economics or political science. We hope that these case studies will provide an appreciation of the complexities entailed in the study of diverse perspectives on the process of large-scale educational change.

John P. Anchan
Winnipeg, Manitoba, Canada
July 8, 2002

References

Allahar, A. L. (1989) *Sociology and the Periphery: Theories & Issues*. Aurora, Ontario: Garamond Press.

Arnold, G. (1994) *The Third World Handbook*. New York: Cassell.

Arnove, R. F. (2001) Comparative and International Education Society (CIES) facing the twenty-first: Challenge and contributions (Presidential Address). *Comparative Education Review*, **45**(4), 477–503.

Beeby, C. E. (1967) *Planning and the Educational Administrator: Fundamentals of Educational Planning*. Paris: UNESCO, International Institute for Educational Planning.

Beeby, C. E. (Ed.) (1969) *Qualitative Aspects of Educational Planning*. Paris: UNESCO, International Institute for Educational Planning.

Bîrzea, C. (1994) *Educational Policies of the Countries in Transition*. Strasbourg: Council of Europe Press.

Carlsson, I. and Ramphal, S. (1995) *Our Global Neighbourhood – The Report of the Commission on Global Governance*. New York: Oxford University Press.

Carnoy, M. (1974) *Education as Cultural Imperialism*. New York: David McKay.

Carnoy, M. and Samoff, J. (1990) *Education and Social Transition in the Third World*. New Jersey: Princeton University Press.

Carter, J. (1997) Post-Fordism and the theorisation of educational change: What's in a name? *British Journal of Sociology of Education*, **18**(1), 45–61.

Eisenstadt, S. N. (1974) Studies of modernization and sociological theory. *History & Theory, Studies in Philosophy of History*, **8**(3).

Freire, P. (1978) *Education for Critical Consciousness*. New York: Seabury Press.

Freire, P. (1983) *Pedagogy of the Oppressed*. New York: Continuum Publishing Corporation.

Freire, P. (1985) *The Politics of Education*. New York: Bergin & Garvey.

Guthrie, G. (1980) Stages of educational development? Beeby revisited. *International Review of Education*, **26**(4), 411–438.

Hurst, P. (1981) Aid and educational development: rhetoric and reality. *Comparative Education*, **17**(2), 117–125.

Hodgkinson, P. (1991) Educational change: a model for its analysis. *British Journal of Sociology of Education*, **12**(2), 203–222.

Larrain, J. (1983) *Marxism and Ideology* [Monograph]. Atlantic Highlands, NJ: Humanities Press.

Larrain, J. (1989) *Theories of Development: Capitalism, Colonialism, and Dependency.* Cambridge, MA: B. Blackwell Inc.

Larrain, J. (1994) *Ideology and Cultural Identity: Modernity and the Third World Presence* [Monograph]. MA: Polity Press.

Larrain, J. (2000) *Identity and Modernity in Latin America.* Malden, Mass.: Polity Press.

Mason, M. (1997) *Development and Disorder: A History of the Third World Since 1945.* Toronto, Canada: Between the Lines.

McLeish, E. (1996) Educational change and social transformation: Teachers, schools and universities in Eastern Germany. *Compare*, **26**(3), 367–369.

Mays, A. (2000) The Initiation and Implementation of Educational Change: The Transformation Process in the Baltic States. In B. T. Peck, and A. Mays (Eds), *Challenge and Change in Education: The Experience of the Baltic States in the 1990s*, (pp. 191–216). Huntington, NY: Nova Science Publishers, Inc.

Peck, B. T. and Mays, A. (Eds) (2000) *Challenge and Change in Education: The Experience of the Baltic States in the 1990s.* Huntington, NY: Nova Science Publishers, Inc.

Shapiro, S. (1998) Beyond the sociology of education: Culture, politics, and the promise of educational change. *Educational Theory*, **38**(4), 415–430.

Sieber, S. D. (1972) Images of the practitioner and strategies of educational change. *Sociology of Education*, **45**, 362–385.

Tharoor, S. (1997) *India: From Midnight to the Millennium.* New York: Arcade Publishing.

Toh, S. H. (1980) *The overseas development council: An elite policy-planning group on U.S.-Third World relations, its power structure and international development-education ideology.* Unpublished doctoral dissertation, University of Alberta, Canada.

Torres, C. A. (2001) Globalization and comparative education in the world system [Editorial]. *Comparative Education Review*, **45**(4), iii-x.

Zakharieva, M. N. (1991) Studying innovations in education: Internationalization of approaches. *Current Sociology*, **39**(1), 119–136.

PREFACE

The key to effective change is to stay poised on [the] ... edge of chaos.

(Brown and Eisenhardt, 1998, p. 14)

McLeish and Phillips, in the introduction to their 1998 publication *Processes of Transition in Education Systems,* acknowledge that 'Very little has been written about post-totalitarian educational transition from a *theoretical* point of view, and thus there is no body of literature upon which to draw in an effort to provide a theoretical construct for the notion of educational transition' (p. 13). While an emerging body of literature is beginning to address recent educational changes in Russia and former-Communist Central and Eastern European countries, many of these studies remain descriptive in nature (see, for example, Furjaeva, 1994; Zajda, 1994; Guseva and Sosnowksi, 1997; Ray, 1997). This book is unique in three ways. First, it examines educational change as a 'process' rather than as an 'event'; second, it explores recent educational changes against a conceptual framework developed by Fullan (2001) for understanding large-scale educational change; and third, it uses the nation as the unit of analysis in which the original impetus for change has occurred, although change at the individual school-district, school, or classroom level is also addressed.

Educational change is examined in five post-Soviet nations: Russia, the Czech Republic, Hungary, Romania, and East Germany. The selection of these countries is based on their contrastive political, social, and economic development following the collapse of communism. For example, transition in the Czech Republic and Hungary was already under way before 1991, but the end of Soviet hegemony cleared a path for change. Romania practised a pure and hard communism, very similar to the Asian model and to original Stalinism, until 1989, when the totalitarian state led by Nicolae Ceauşescu was brought down in a violent and bloody revolution (Bîrzea, 1995). East Germany was the only country in Eastern Europe to be absorbed into another (the Federal Republic of Germany). In Russia, where communist ideology, born of the 1917 Bolshevik Revolution, emerged from *within* (unlike former Soviet-Bloc countries, upon which communism was imposed from without), dissent was swiftly eliminated through widespread executions and imprisonment, especially during the Stalin era. The comparative perspective which this book provides across these five different former Soviet-satellite countries adds depth and interpretive power to the analysis.

In this book, we have sought to illuminate some important features of the forces that shape sudden and dramatic large-scale educational reform, and to suggest new directions in the study of educational change with the potential to guide strategic planning of the transformation of education in societies where change is profound and rapid. We hope that this book contributes to scholarly discourse on educational reform and to recent conceptual developments in complexity theory.

References

Arnove, R. F. (2001) Comparative and International Education Society (CIES) facing the twenty-first: challenge and contributions (Presidential Address). *Comparative Education Review*, **45**(4), 477–503.

Bîrzea, C. (1995) Educational reform and educational research in Central-Eastern Europe: the case of Romania. Paper presented at the IBE International Meeting on Educational Reform and Educational Research, Tokyo, Japan.

Brown, S. and Eisenhardt, K. (1998) *Competing on the Edge*, Boston, MA: Harvard Business School Press.

Fullan, M. (2001) *The New Meaning of Educational Change* (3rd edn). New York: Teachers College Press.

Furjaeva, T. (1994) Children and youth in the policy, science and practice of a society. In V.D. Rust, P. Knost and J. Wichmann (Eds), *Education and the Values Crisis in Central and Eastern Europe* (pp. 131–157). Frankfurt, Germany: Peter Lang.

Guseva, L. and Sosnowski, A. (1997) Russian education in transition: trends at the primary level. *Canadian and International Education*, **26**(1), 14–31.

McLeish, A. and Phillips, D. (1998) *Processes of Transition in Education System* (Series: *Oxford Studies in Comparative Education*), **8**(2). Wallingford, Oxfordshire: Symposium Books.

Ray, F. (1997) Russian-Canadian cooperation in curriculum development: Russian civic education, 1990–1996. *Canadian and International Education*, **26**(1), 1–13.

Zajda, J. (1994) Educational reforms and the discourse of democracy in Soviet and post-communist education: evidence from a Meta-Analysis. *International Perspectives on Education and Society*, **4**, 165–203.

ACKNOWLEDGEMENTS

The editors would like to acknowledge a number of individuals who have helped bring this book to life. Special thanks are due to the authors of each case study: Eduard Dneprov, Marie Černá, Gábor Halász, Cesar Bîrzea, Ciprian Fartuşnic, and Nina Arnhold, whose contributions have allowed us to extend our knowledge of large-scale educational reform from both theoretical and practical perspectives. Their reflections on the process of educational change in their own countries are distinguished not only by their unique insights but also by the sense of moral purpose and enduring optimism manifest in their writing. Heartfelt thanks also go to Reena Kreindler for her invaluable editorial advice and thoughtful suggestions for revisions which helped focus, tighten, and strengthen the manuscript – she was literally a partner in producing this book. Finally, we would like to thank our families, whose patience, support, and belief in the book from the time it was first conceived have sustained us through the many long hours of work which have gone into shaping this volume – it was well worth it! We hope this final product contributes to the academic discourse on educational change theory among members of the international and comparative education community, in a way that is commensurate with at least a fraction of the support we have received.

Part I

UNDERSTANDING LARGE-SCALE REFORM

1

THE DYNAMIC FORCES OF CHANGE

Michael Fullan
Ontario Institute for Studies in Education
University of Toronto

Understanding the forces of educational change in post-Communist central Europe is a complex matter, as the ensuing chapters demonstrate. We can, however, start with a rather simple model in order to organize ideas to represent the flow of educational change. In this chapter, I present the model and supplement it with several additional 'change issues' that all large-scale systems must address in the transformation process. I start with the framework itself – the Triple I model (Fullan, 2001a).

The Triple I model

The number and dynamics of factors that interact and affect the process of educational change are too overwhelming to compute in anything resembling a fully determined way. We do know more about the processes of change as a result of research of the past 30 years, which has shown that there are no hard-and-fast rules, but rather a set of suggestions or implications given the contingencies specific to local situations. In fact, Clark *et al.* (1984), Huberman and Miles (1984), Fullan (1999), and others suggest that the uniqueness of the individual setting is a critical factor – what works in one situation may or may not work in another. This is not to say that there are not guidelines, and we will get to them. Research findings on the change process should be used less as instruments of 'application' and more as means of helping practitioners and planners 'make sense' of planning, implementation strategies, and monitoring. It is also important to say that this is a feasible task: 'Schools, classrooms, and school systems can and do improve and the factors facilitating improvement are neither so exotic, unusual, or expensive that they are beyond the grasp of … ordinary schools' (Clark *et al.*, 1984, pp. 59, 66).

Most researchers now see three broad phases to the change process. Phase I – variously labelled initiation, mobilization, or adoption – consists of the process that leads up to and includes a decision to adopt or proceed with a change. Phase II – implementation or initial use (usually the first two or three years of use) – involves the first experiences of attempting to put an idea or reform into practice. Phase III – called continuation, incorporation, routinization, or institutionalization – refers to whether the change gets built in as an ongoing part of the system or disappears by way of a decision to discard or through attrition (see Berman and McLaughlin, 1977; Huberman and Miles, 1984). Figure 1 depicts the three phases in relation to outcomes, especially whether or not student learning is enhanced, and whether or not experiences with change increase subsequent capacity to deal with future changes.

In simple terms, an individual or group for whatever reason initiates or promotes a certain programme or direction of change. The direction of change, which may be more or less defined at the early stages, moves to a phase of attempted use (implementation), which can be more or less effective. Continuation is an extension of the implementation phase in that the new programme is sustained beyond the first year or two (or whatever time frame is chosen). Outcome, depending on the objectives, can refer to several different types of results and can generally be thought of as the degree of school improvement in relation to given criteria. Results could include, for example, improved student learning and attitudes; new skills, attitudes, or satisfaction on the part of teachers and other school personnel; or improved problem-solving capacity of the school as an organization.

Figure 1 presents only the general image of a much more detailed and snarled process. First, there are numerous factors operating at each phase. Second, as the two-way arrows imply, it is not a linear process but rather one in which events at one phase can feed back to alter decisions made at previous stages, which then proceed to work their way through in a continuous interactive way. For example, a decision at the initiation phase to use a specific programme may be substantially modified during implementation, and so on.

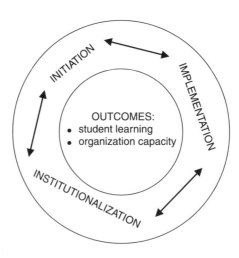

Figure 1 A simplified overview of the change process.

The third set of variables, which are unspecified in Figure 1, concerns the scope of change and the question of who develops and initiates the change. The scope can range from large-scale externally developed innovations to locally produced ones. In either of these cases the teacher may or may not be centrally involved in development and/or decisions to proceed. Thus, the concept of 'initiation' leaves open the question of who develops or initiates the change.

The fourth complication in Figure 1 is that the total time perspective as well as sub-phases cannot be precisely demarcated. The initiation phase may be in the works for years, but even later specific decision-making and pre-implementation planning activities can be lengthy. Implementation for most changes takes two or more years; only then can we consider change to have really had a chance to become implemented. The line between implementation and continuation is somewhat hazy and arbitrary. Outcomes can be assessed in the relatively short run, but we would not expect much in the way of results until the change has had a chance to become implemented. In this sense, implementation is the *means* to achieving certain outcomes; evaluations have limited value and can be misleading if they provide information on outcomes only.

The total time frame from initiation to institutionalization is lengthy: even moderately complex changes take from three to five years, while larger-scale efforts may take five to ten years and still experience difficulty in sustaining improvements. The single most important idea is that *change is a process, not an event* – a lesson learned the hard way by those who put all their energies into developing an innovation or passing a piece of legislation without thinking through what will have to happen beyond that point.

So far, we have been talking as if schools adopt one innovation at a time. This single-innovation perspective can be useful for examining individual innovations, but the broader reality, of course, is that schools are in the business of contending simultaneously with *multiple innovations* or innovation overload. Thus, when we identify factors affecting successful initiation and implementation, we should think of these factors as operating across many innovations – and many levels of the system (classroom, school, district, state, nation). This multiplicity perspective inevitably leads one to look for solutions at the level of individual roles and groups. This is so because it is only at the individual and small group level that the inevitable demands of overload can be prioritized and integrated. At the same time, we should try to achieve great policy alignment at the state level.

What happens at one stage of the change process strongly affects subsequent stages, but new determinants also appear. It should also be understood that all three phases should be considered at the outset. As one goes about the initiation of change, implementation planning must already be under way. Put another way, the moment that initiating begins is the moment that the stage is being set for implementation and continuation.

Mainly to illustrate the kinds of factors important at each stage, Figure 2 lists the eight factors we have identified as critical at the initiation or beginning stage.

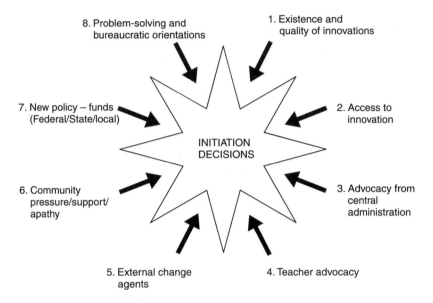

Figure 2 Factors affecting initiation.

How change gets started involves a crucial set of factors. Contrary to popular opinion, 'ownership' or democratic participation in change decisions is not the typical starting point. As we shall see, ownership must develop over time (over the stages of implementation and institutionalization), but usually cannot be achieved at the first stage. The latter often requires assertive leadership or policy initiation. Thus, in addition to 'the existence and quality of innovations' and 'access to innovations', advocacy must arise from one or several sources: central administration (factor 3), teachers (factor 4), external change agents (factor 5), community pressure (factor 6), and/or new policy initiatives (factor 7). Also important is whether the initiators have a strong commitment to solving a major problem, as distinguished from a bureaucratic or superficial political reason for taking on the appearance, but not necessarily the substance, of reform (factor 8).

Once change gets started, a series of conditions must exist or be developed to support and monitor actual implementation. Implementation concerns the motivation, skills, beliefs and resources essential for putting new ideas into practice. Figure 3 lists the nine characteristics which we have found to play a role in fostering or inhibiting implementation.

The innovation or reform policy itself must address an existing or potential need; it must be clear enough to be pursued; it can be complex as long as enough time and resources are devoted to sorting out the complexity; and it must be developed with increasing quality and practicality for use. A second set of implementation factors concerns local characteristics or capacities (again – motiva-

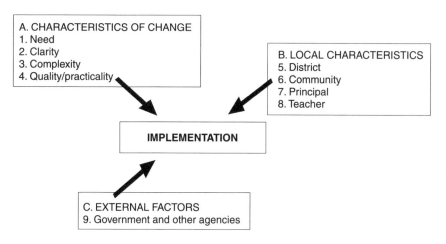

Figure 3 Interactive factors affecting implementation.

tion, skill, beliefs) on the part of districts or regions, community, principals and teachers. A third set involves the role of state and national government and other societal agencies.

The final phase – continuation – is a matter of building the innovation or policy into more permanent structures, formal policies, incentive systems, and training for newcomers as well as continuous training at all levels.

The Triple I model has served us well in analysing innovations and policies, and is indeed used productively in several chapters in this book. There are three additional problems I would like to introduce at this point (and to which we will return in the final chapter of the book):

1   the multiple innovations or coherence-making problem;
2   maintaining the balance between and integration of pressure and support strategies; and
3   building new infrastructures.

Multiple innovations

The Triple I model was originally developed to apply to single (albeit, major) innovations or policies. The reality is that societal transformation involves multiple innovations occurring simultaneously and not usually in concert. An endemic problem for all major reforms is that they are nonlinear, often piecemeal, and represent tremendous overload and confusion for most implementers (Fullan, 1999, 2001b). We need then to understand how multiple, disconnected innovations can be made to cohere and otherwise work in a more integrated fashion. As I have argued elsewhere, this is not a problem that can be solved once and for all (Fullan, 2001b); yet it is essential and possible to work effectively on 'the coherence-making problem'. In a study of complex education policies in England, Wallace and Pocklington (in press) applied the Triple I model in order to help us understand how complex policies unfold. They added one additional framework that provided a powerful complement to the Triple I model. They suggest that one should focus on the three phases, but that four additional overriding change themes must be addressed in order to take into account the dynamic nonlinear nature of change factors. In particular, they identify the following themes:

1   the metatask of coordination across many groups;
2   flexible planning and coordination;
3   culture building and communication; and
4   differentiated support in order to build greater capacity where it is needed.

These themes strengthen the applicability of the Triple I model when we are examining transformation of whole systems as distinct from tracing single innovations.

Pressure and support

Another critical theme that runs through our analysis of large-scale reform concerns the sophisticated blend of pressure and support; or, as we have called it more recently, accountability and capacity-building. Pressure or accountability involves new mandates, achievement targets, monitoring, publication of results, and even new forms of implementers interacting while focusing on results (thereby creating peer or lateral accountability). Support or capacity-building concerns new resources, training, new leadership roles, materials, and other forms of interactive skill development. England, for example, is deliberately and systematically employing such a pressure and support set of strategies in order to improve literacy and numeracy in its over 19,000 primary schools (see Fullan, 2001a, Chapter 13). The results have been amazing. From 1996 (the baseline just prior to the employment of the strategy) to 2001, the percentage of 11-year-olds in the entire country who achieved proficiency in literacy moved from 57 per cent to 75 per cent; for mathematics the gain was from 54 per cent to 71 per cent. So, major reform involves establishing a sophisticated blend of pressure and support mechanisms.

Infrastructure

The third set of requirements consists of the creation of new infrastructure capacities. Since the early 1990s, most systems have turned their attention to large-scale, sustainable reform. It was earlier thought that local school and community development was the answer. It still is. But the new insight is that you cannot get local development on any scale unless the larger infrastructure is strengthened. This means that district or regional capacities for leading and supporting change

8

THE DYNAMIC FORCES OF CHANGE

must be developed; agencies involved in the initial and continuing training of teachers must be strengthened; new strategies and mechanisms for leadership development at all levels (teacher leaders, principals, superintendents, etc.) must be established; and agencies to develop and maintain curricular materials and to monitor and report on progress (e.g. student achievement levels) must be put into place.

All in all, we have accumulated a good deal of knowledge about large-scale educational reform. The case studies of educational and societal transformation in post-Communist Eastern Europe provide a rich and critical opportunity to add to and expand this growing knowledge base.

References

Berman, P. and McLaughlin, M. (1977) *Federal Programs Supporting Educational Change: Vol. 7. Factors Affecting Implementation and Continuation.* Santa Monica, CA: Rand Corporation.

Clark, D., Lotto, S. and Astuto, T. (1984) Effective schools and school improvement: a comparative analysis of two lines of inquiry. *Educational Administration Quarterly*, **20**(3), 41–68.

Fullan, M. (1999) *Change Forces.* London: The Falmer Press.

Fullan, M. (2001a) *The New Meaning of Educational Change* (3rd edn). New York: Teachers College Press.

Fullan, M. (2001b) *Leading in a Culture of Change.* San Francisco: Jossey Bass.

Huberman, M. and Miles, M. (1984) *Innovation Up Close.* New York: Plenum.

Wallace, M. and Pocklington, K. (2002) *Managing Complex Educational Change: Large-scale Reorganisation of Schools.* London: RoutledgeFalmer.

Part II

SELECTED CASE STUDIES

2

HARNESSING THE FORCES OF CHANGE

Educational transformation in Russia[1]

Eleoussa Polyzoi, University of Winnipeg, Manitoba, Canada
Eduard Dneprov,[2] University of the Russian Academy of Education,
Moscow, Russia; Former Minister of Education of the Russian
Federation

Scope and objectives

In 1991, the Communist government of the Soviet Union collapsed, and, one after another, the Soviet Republics – including Georgia, Moldavia, White Russia, the Baltic States and the Ukraine – began to secede from the Union. The main priority of the new Russian government, under the leadership of President Boris Yeltsin, was to move from a planned to a free-market economy within a new democratic framework. The new government also promised to initiate significant educational reform. At first, educational change across republics, united by their collective rejection of the communist ideology, was characterized by a striking uniformity. However, as each republic began to chart its own course, their education-reform agendas increasingly began to take on a distinct character (Rust *et al.*, 1994).

As Bîrzea (1994) notes in his analysis of the transition of post-Soviet nations from a totalitarian to an open and democratic system, one of the easiest ways to fill the vacuum not yet filled by new self-regulating mechanisms is to look to the past, to seek out old securities in the face of an uncertain future. However, as Anweiler (1992) cautions, 'The emerging new systems of education in the post-communist societies cannot simply start their reconstruction at the status-quo ante, before the communist regime came to power. This is particularly true in

1   This study was funded by the Social Sciences and Humanities Research Council (SSHRC) internal University of Winnipeg grant. The authors would like to thank the individuals who participated in the study and who gave so generously of their time.

2   Although E. Polyzoi is the primary author of this chapter, the information presented here is based on extensive discussions with and contributions by E. Dneprov whose intimate knowledge of the educational reform process in Russia and unique insights have been invaluable.

the case of Russia and the rest of the former Soviet Union with over 70 years of communist rule behind them' (p. 38). Russia's experience with change has been particularly chaotic and protracted in nature. The events of 1991 set the stage for a major contradiction within the Russian educational system. The inconsistency between the overwhelming administrative rigidity, which was a legacy of the centralized Communist educational structure, and the new principles of democracy made change inevitable.

The objective of this chapter is to explore the *initiation* of educational transformation in Russia since 1991 within the context of a framework of educational change proposed by Michael Fullan (1993, 1999, 2001).[3] Since educational transformation in Russia has unfolded within a more compressed time frame than in North America, the Russia experience provides a unique opportunity for the investigation of educational change – a 'living laboratory', qualitatively different from the United States or Canada where change occurs within an essentially stable societal context.

We argue that Fullan's conceptual framework does have utility for helping us understand events in Russia; however, we propose a revised framework which better accounts for the dynamic character of dramatic and sudden change typical of Russia and other former Soviet-satellite countries.

Fullan's conceptual framework – a focus on the initiation of change

According to Fullan (2001), most researchers acknowledge three broad phases to the process of educational change: *initiation, implementation,* and *institutionalization* (see Part I of this book). The current examination – the first in a series of five case studies presented in this volume – focuses on the *initiation* of change in Russia since 1991. Initiation consists of the process that leads up to and includes a decision to adopt an idea or reform into practice. Fullan identifies the following eight factors (taken from the literature) as affecting initiation:

1 advocacy from central administration;
2 bureaucratic orientations and problem-solving approaches;
3 teacher advocacy;
4 new policy/funds at the federal, state and local levels;
5 existence and quality of innovations;
6 community pressure/support or apathy;
7 access to information; and
8 external change agents.

---

3 This study represents the replication and expansion of a three-year study examining educational change in the Czech Republic (Mays *et al.,* 1997).

The authors examine each of these factors in detail in an attempt to understand the extent to which initiation of educational transformation in Russia has taken place and the characteristics of such change within the context of Fullan's framework.[4]

Method/data sources

The information in this chapter is based on lengthy interviews which the principal author conducted in Moscow between March and April 1999. Interviews were conducted with 24 key individuals, selected because of their key roles in the educational system and its transformation. Interviewees included members of the Ministry of Education, teacher educators, university researchers, and members of advocacy and school reform organizations. The authors deliberately selected this wide variety of participants, in accordance with the concept of 'shared meaning of change' (Fullan, 2001, p. 9). A number of interviewees also furnished important primary (government, policy, and school) documents related to the change process of educational transformation; these documents address selected innovative programmes, provide statistical data on various aspects of the education system, and describe legislative changes that have been introduced in Russia since 1991.

The authors acknowledge that this study is based on research conducted in a small geographical area (Moscow) and with a restricted number of interviewees. Furthermore, the interpretations of events reflect the authors' own perspectives, which unavoidably are influenced both by the viewpoints of the interviewees and by the specific period in time. Nevertheless, in the short time available, a wealth of primary information was collected from individuals who played a significant role in the reform movement in Moscow, particularly during Russia's initial transition period.

The format for the interviews involved a common open-ended, unstructured questionnaire, upon which the researcher elaborated with additional probe questions as the interview unfolded. The interviews ranged from one to two hours in length; approximately 50–55 hours of interviews were recorded on audiocassettes. About one quarter of the interviewees spoke English; the services of an interpreter (a journalism student from Moscow State University) were used in those cases in which the interviewee spoke only Russian. Data analyses involved examination of the transcribed interviews and extensive notes and documents acquired by the principal researcher. The Russian experience was then matched against the *initiation* stage of Fullan's framework in order to understand Russia's transformation as a 'change' process.

The context – public discontent with an education system in need of restructuring

The genesis of education reform in the USSR does not date from the dissolution of the Soviet Union; it began much earlier. When Mikhail Gorbachev came to

---

4   In addition, it suggests an extension to the framework which addresses more clearly the dynamic elements of sudden change.

power in 1985, it was becoming increasingly clear that the Soviet education system was in need of restructuring. As reported in the Russian newspaper, *Izvestia* (December 1988, p. 3), the whole country had 'slipped onto the sidelines of world progress scientifically, technologically, economically and socially'.

During the decade preceding *perestroika*, Russian education was characterized by a marked decline in the quality of teachers and teacher training, authoritarian and inflexible teaching methods, a static and bureaucratic administrative structure which left little room for teacher initiative, and outdated textbooks whose content was overlaid with increasingly discredited communist ideology. In addition, research and development, related to the reality of teaching was almost nonexistent, and teachers' working conditions were abysmal: teachers' salaries were lower than those of industrial skilled workers, basic school supplies were difficult to obtain, and school buildings (particularly in the rural areas) lacked running water, central heating, and indoor plumbing (Kerr, 1991, 1995). These conditions prompted a re-examination of the Russian education system and precipitated the initiation of major change.

In 1984, one year before becoming leader of the Communist Party, Mikhail Gorbachev served as chairman of a commission examining educational reform. This commission's recommendations included the national establishment of a compulsory computer-literacy course at the high school level; the improvement of in-service training programmes, and minimal raises in teacher salaries. However, these 'muted' measures were characterized as nothing more than reform 'by the bureaucrats for the bureaucrats' (Kerr, 1991). By 1987, Gorbachev had begun talking openly about his programme of *perestroika* in terms of a revolutionary shift in how Soviet citizens were to begin thinking about themselves and their role in the world. During this early period, the education media – particularly the *Teachers Gazette* (*Uchitel'skaia gazetta*), edited by V. F. Matveev – played a critical role in supporting a spontaneous grass-roots campaign that questioned the fundamental assumptions underlying the Soviet education system. The education media, a barometer of teachers' sentiments, became an important means through which community pressure for change was exerted (Nechaev, 1999).[5]

Between 1987 and 1989, against a backdrop of increasing public complaint, several main developments took place which pushed the education debate forward. First, in 1987, Eduard Dneprov, a maverick educational reformer, founded a semi-autonomous School Ad Hoc Research Group (VNIK-SHKOLA) to develop a new 'conception' of general education (Dneprov, 1999a). Second, a new Creative Teachers Union (independent of the state-sponsored educators' trade union) was founded which gave teachers a more forceful professional voice and the

---

5   The newspaper regularly printed critiques by teachers, school administrators, prominent intellectuals, and scientists, and served as a critical venue for public expression and dialogue (Dimova, 1999).

potential to affect national policy. Third, the structure of educational research and development in the USSR (which had been within the purview of the Academy of Pedagogical Sciences and its constituent research institutes) was subjected to a major overhaul in order to make allocation of contracts more equitable, research output more productive, and the quality of studies more responsive to educators' current needs (Kerr, 1990).

However, the old bureaucratic counter forces in education turned out to be too strong and resistant to change. Although the long-awaited meeting of the Congress of Education Workers in December 1988 proved that many teachers supported the position outlined by VNIK-SHKOLA (Dneprov, 1999a), real power still remained in the hands of conservatives. The visionary proposals introduced in 1998 by Dneprov's VNIK group were so carefully scrutinized and repeatedly rewritten by the bureaucracy that it became difficult to recognize their original liberal thrust. Matveev and his reform-minded colleagues were forced out of the *Teachers Gazette* in 1989. The reform movement had minimal representation on the newly created Council on National Education. The expected reform of the Academy of Pedagogical Sciences did not take place. The old guard had succeeded in obstructing any plans for major educational reorganization.

The direction of the political winds in the USSR, however, was not always predictable. In 1991, the Soviet Union dissolved; Boris Yeltsin became leader of the new Russian Socialist Federated Soviet Republic (RSFSR), and the education critic and reformist Dneprov was suddenly catapulted into the role of RSFSR Minister of Education, bringing with him the small team of reformers who had founded VNIK-SHKOLA. In his first few days in office, Dneprov fired hundreds of officials and moved swiftly to introduce his new conception of education (Kerr, 1991). Key terms such as 'humanization', 'differentiation', 'democratization', and 'pluralization' defined the guiding principles of this vision (Rust, 1992).

After the introduction of the Law on Education in 1992 (slightly revised in 1996), the government said little on educational matters. However, many gaps remained in the federal laws, regulations, and policies governing education, and regional and local policies became even more diverse, creating an increasingly confusing and chaotic situation. In the summer of 1997, the government announced a new programme of educational reform. The announcement was eagerly anticipated by Russian teachers, administrators, educational consultants/ entrepreneurs, as well as central bureaucrats (Kerr, 1998). Teachers were angry about salary arrears and concerned about the effects of social and economic upheaval on their schools. Administrators were confounded by unfamiliar financial procedures and uncertain about their legal authority. Educational consultants/ entrepreneurs were anxious about the lack of federal and regional support for truly new educational approaches and fearful of a return to a centralized system. Central bureaucrats were infuriated by the increasing educational autonomy of the regions, and apprehensive about the potential impact that regional diversity might have on higher education (Kerr, 1998). Initially, the Commission responsible for drafting the new reform proposal expressed a desire to reaffirm the principles articulated in the original work of the VNIK-SHKOLA under Dneprov's leadership. However, in the autumn of 1997, stronger centrist factions emerged within the Commission; by December, educational financing and the payment of educators' back salaries became overriding issues. Further action on the reform proposals was delayed by the Duma in May 1998 following strikes staged by teachers, students, and professors in sympathy with the Siberian miners' demonstrations. The final version of the reform document clearly favoured a more conservative vision and one oriented primarily toward economic concerns (Kerr, 1998).

The case: an analysis of the initiation of educational change in Russia

In considering educational reform in Russia, one must acknowledge the complex historical legacy of the Soviet education system. Soviet education was characterized by a rigid, federally controlled, common school curriculum which emphasized the acquisition of factual knowledge in highly specialized subjects and left little room for individual pedagogical initiatives; textbooks were provided by a state publication monopoly and educational needs were guided by a centralized manpower planning strategy. Since the dissolution of the Soviet Union, the nation has been influenced by a plethora of competing social, political, and economic forces – sometimes enabling educational change, sometimes derailing or obstructing it – but always dynamic in character.

What follows is a discussion of Fullan's eight-factor schema as it applies to the Russian experience of the initiation of change. Since the landscape of education reform in Russia is so remarkably complex, this discussion will focus on one of the most pressing issues identified by the OECD team in their 1998 report, namely, the decentralization of the Russian education system. The 1992 Law on Education (and subsequent amendments) has provided the legislative framework for this major policy shift. Although tensions unavoidably accompanied the decentralization effort, it was widely believed by Russians that only through such restructuring could innovative ideas, curricula, teaching methods, and programmes evolve. Although the following analysis is not to be understood as precluding other related levels of reform, it will necessarily assume a macro-perspective, and change will be considered primarily at the national level rather than at the level of school division, school, or classroom.

Advocacy from central administration/bureaucratic orientations – laying the foundation for a new educational vision

According to Fullan (2001, p. 58), 'initiation of change never occurs without an advocate, and one of the most powerful [of these] is the chief district administrator ... [however] ... administrators can be equally powerful at blocking change'. In Russia, although one cannot credit any single individual with the role of chief advocate, it is clear that strong advocates of educational change exerted

18

influence at the highest level of government; the most influential of these were Eduard Dneprov and his reform group. Before his 1990 appointment as Minister of Education, Dneprov realized that radical change of the education system was necessary in order to adapt to the emergent forces of democratization and liberalization, to develop civic education and students' capacity for critical thinking. To this end, Dneprov's allies sought to break the totalitarian bureaucracy and to rapidly 'de-monopolize' and 'decentralize' administrative and curricular authority. The New Law on Education, ushered in by Dneprov in 1992, laid the foundation for a new vision of education in Russia.

However, just as there were early forces that advocated for reform from central administration, there were also counter forces that made its realization difficult. Although Dneprov's 1992 Law on Education was seen by some as an enormous accomplishment, others took a different view. According to Johnson (1997), Dneprov's insistence on a 'big bang' to force the reform through was perceived as a politically questionable strategy. The rapid decentralization thus prematurely initiated only served to aggravate administrative and financial chaos at the regional and local levels. Faced with bitter resistance and increasingly caustic personal and political attacks from conservative educators, Dneprov was forced to resign as Minister of Education in December 1992.

In Russia, the factors 'advocacy from central administration' and 'bureaucratic orientations' appear to be intimately linked. Fullan defines the latter as the perspective brought by central administrators to the decision to introduce an innovation or change. Such adoption decisions may be characterized either by an opportunistic (bureaucratic) approach or by a genuine problem-solving orientation that responds to a real need. Cynics might argue that reform in Russia was introduced by bureaucrats motivated by political expediency. Others might claim that the true driving force behind Dneprov's reform movement was a strong sense of 'moral purpose' (Fullan, 1999), a desire to modernize the inefficient Russian education system. There is probably some truth to both views. Pinski adds a further layer of explanation: 'The "winds of freedom" in the early 1990s helped push Dneprov's new conception of education through. However, the principles embodied in his law lacked the details needed to effectively transform the system' (Pinski, 1999). Dneprov, realizing the urgency of consolidating his 'conception' into law, hoped that its framework would be fleshed out at a later time through a series of amendments. However, this became increasingly difficult as economic conditions rapidly deteriorated and the Duma's conservative elements gained influence. In what Dneprov refers to as the 'Communist revenge', the Communist majority succeeded in blocking further attempts at educational reform (Dneprov, 1999a).[6] At the time of this writing (spring, 2000), Russia was preparing for national elections; and although a Communist government was considered a

---

6 Johnson (1997) observes that the 'politics of personality based on arcane and bitter personal rivalries and ambitions' within Russian bureaucracy impede attempts to advance reform (p. 223).

(Contd)

possibility, many believed that a return to the former Soviet model of education was now an impossibility.[7]

Role of teachers unions/teacher advocacy – the birth of Russia's educational reform movement

Fullan acknowledges that national teacher unions in North America have become strong advocates of reform, and indeed can be powerful initiators; however, he cautions, 'most teachers do not have adequate information, access, time or energy [to initiate changes]; and the innovations they do adopt are often individualistic [rather than broad-based or wide-reaching]' (Fullan, 2001, p. 60). The implication is that advocacy from district administrators and/or union leaders is necessary for district-wide changes.

The official teachers trade union that existed for many years in the Soviet Union was never seen by Russian teachers as an organization that served their interests, but rather as a government agency of control (Krugliakov, 1999). The *perestroika* period saw the emergence of over 400 independent teacher organizations, whose common interest was to engage teachers in discussion about new forms of education which collectively came to be known as the *pedagogy of cooperation* – perceiving the teacher as guide rather than taskmaster, treating students with respect, engaging in honest dialogue with other teachers, encouraging variety in teaching, etc. (Kerr, 1991). Many of these organizations soon adopted the name 'Eureka Club', and a new movement was born, led by journalist and physics teacher Alexander Adamsky. By 1988, the *Teachers Gazette* began to provide wide coverage of the clubs' activities. Shortly thereafter, the clubs banded together to form the Creative Union of Teachers, which ultimately included most of the country's well-known innovators and activists, including S. Lysenkova,

The controversial OECD Background Report (Bolotov, 1995) is one example that merits some attention: In October 1995, a team of experts at the Ministry of Education, in response to a request by the OECD team, prepared a background document which provided a candid analysis of accomplishments, mistakes, and new challenges in Russian education. However, despite its professional nature, the survey and its authors were viciously attacked in an incident that seems to have been linked to political struggles within the education establishment. '… the attacks were full of insinuations and innuendo about personal motivations that reminded some observers of the … form of political denunciation perfected in Soviet time. The most serious charge was that its distribution represented an attempt to discredit the Yeltsin government in the eyes of the West and undermine him in his race for president of the Federation' (Vaillant, 1997, p. 3). As a result, the distribution of the background report was limited and controversial information deliberately left out of the final OECD report prepared by the official European examination team (Lenskaya, 1999).

7 On March 26, 2000, Vladimir Putin, former Head of the KGB, was elected president of the Russian Federation. His military successes in the Chechnyan war made him immensely popular among Russians who felt that he could effectively guide the country out of its economic turmoil. Appointed as Yeltsin's successor, Putin believed that Russia could move forward only if it combined the principles of a market economy and democracy with the realities of Russian history, culture and society.

V. Davydov, B. Bim-Bad, V. Karakovskii and A. Tubelski (Kerr, 1991). Upon gaining legal status in the spring of 1989, the Creative Union began to link with foreign groups such as *Phi Delta Kappan* in the USA; and, by the early 1990s, emerged as an important provider of in-service training for Soviet teachers. Eureka illustrates a phenomenon unique to the USSR: an independent approach to in-service delivery – training created for teachers by the teachers themselves. By fall 1991, several thousand teachers had participated in Eureka seminars offered throughout the country (Kerr, 1991). The difficulty of teacher unions in Russia to effectively mobilize their members (Johnson, 1997) is understandable considering the fact that political consciousness was hardly nurtured during the Communist era. Nevertheless, the sporadic strikes in the spring of 1995, the one-day national strike in the fall of the same year, as well as the recent strikes which immediately preceded the economic crisis of August 1998 have demonstrated some nascent, albeit minimal, political consciousness among teachers.

It is indisputable that the Creative Union of Teachers succeeded in energizing more reform-minded educators, who, in turn, had the potential to effect change in their own schools. However, escalating economic hardships and the realization that the reform measures would ultimately require a complete 're-culturing' of the education system (Fullan, 1993)[8] forced many teachers to pull back, despite early enthusiasm for the principles of democratic education and the 'pedagogy of cooperation'. The government's 1997 announcement of its new programme of educational renewal was met with significant resistance. As one educator angrily commented in a front page editorial of the *Teachers Gazette* (No. 51, Dec. 23, 1997, as reported in Elkof, 1997): 'We are swamped by a tidal wave of catastrophes ... crushing debts, salaries unpaid for months on end, work stoppages and hunger strikes ... And what have we here – yet more reform? ...Will reform bring the school its long-lost revenues, or take away its remaining kopeks? Will reform help us cope with the deception we have experienced; can we take yet more empty promises seriously?' To teachers who felt betrayed by the government, the word 'reform' had become anathema by 1998 (Pinksi, 1999). The teacher's situation is complicated by the deteriorating conditions of the schools (collapsing facilities, lack of material supplies, minimal funds for capital repairs), as well as by the serious physical health problems experienced by the majority of students in Russian schools (for example, many children come to school physically weak due to malnourishment; others have vision problems, serious tooth decay, skeletal deformities, and heart and circulatory problems

---

8   Teachers were beset with a whole complex of confusing, often competing, new demands. For example, they were required to be more accountable to parents and administrators, who began increasingly to question their work (Krugliakov, 1999). The steadily growing influx of new curricular materials challenged teachers unused to making independent decisions about instructional design and curriculum development. The new law and its host of legal requirements (for example, the regular evaluation of teachers' work and of school accreditation) introduced new pressures and placed increasing burdens on teachers (Kerr, 1995).

(Kerr, 1996)). In addition, the continued exodus of young, bright teachers and the consequent aging of the teaching body aggravate an already critical situation (Kerr, 1996).

New policy/funds to support decentralization – inadequate local capacity-building

One of the major elements of the 1992 Law on Education was the devolution of selected administrative and fiscal responsibilities from central to regional and local authorities. In moving towards a decentralized system, it is necessary, Fullan warns, to 'strike a balance between too little and too much structure' (Fullan, 1999, p. 51). Too much structure produces rigid rules, highly channelled communication, loss of flexibility, and stunted innovation; too little structure, on the other hand, promotes rule-breaking, loose relationships, random communication, and confusion. The analogy by Brown and Eisenhardt (as cited in Fullan, 1999, p. 5) illustrates this principle well: 'If there are no lights, traffic is chaotic. If there are too many lights, traffic stops. A moderate number of lights creates structure but still allows drivers to adapt their routes in surprising ways in response to changing traffic conditions.' One might argue that in Russia there was too little structure, that the groundwork for effective decentralization was not adequately prepared. Fullan (1999, p. 56) emphasizes the importance of 'local capacity building' as a prerequisite to successful change. He defines this as 'directly and indirectly providing opportunities for advancing the knowledge, skills and work of local school and district personnel [in order to] create powerful learning communities' (p. 57). He admonishes, 'Knowledge ... must be developed not borrowed ... capacity building includes the continual flow and integration of the best ideas available ... rather than the transfer of products' (pp. 68–9). In Russia, legislation was enacted *before* the regions had a chance to develop appropriate decentralized administrative structures for its effective implementation (OECD, 1998, p. 27).[9] As a result, the system was beleaguered by lack of financial coordination, legislative ambiguity, and administrative inexperience. All new administrative obligations devolved to the regions; yet most regions had limited skills in management, budgetary planning, negotiating with teachers unions, defining the new roles of city and district education heads, and identifying the re-training needs of teachers. Although they could not legally refuse their new responsibilities, some regions learned to outwardly conform to the official decentralization policy without truly changing. While there were some success stories

9 Fullan (1993) distinguishes between cultural change (norms, habits, skills, and beliefs) and structural change (physical environment, organizational arrangements, roles, finance governance, curriculum training, etc.). Although 'reculturing is much more difficult than restructuring' (Fullan, 1999, p. 66), change in one domain typically serves as a catalyst for change in the other.

of regional and local self-management, there were also failures involving problems ranging from wage misappropriation to bureaucratic conflict and inertia (OECD, 1998, p. 46). This situation seriously threatened public confidence in the law and raised doubts about the authority of a federal government, which passes legislation it can neither implement nor enforce (OECD, 1998, pp. 35–6).[10]

Fullan also points out that any new policy must be accompanied by sufficient funding to ensure its effective initiation. In Russia, the funding required to support the decentralization of the education system was not fully coordinated with budgetary capacity. Regions (some less affluent than others) were left to pay for educational programmes which the federal government was simply unable to support. Tax administration in Russia is typically 'bottom-up', i.e. revenues are collected locally and may be withheld at that level. Regional authorities, therefore, were in a position to bargain over revenues to be released to the federal government, using their control over local resources and tax revenue as leverage (OECD, 1998, p. 35). However, regions had few incentives to forward tax revenues to the federal government (OECD, 1998, p. 36). Education was often pitted against other social programmes for available funds. Regional inequities intensified emergent local disparities in the quality of education (OECD, 1998, p. 37). Paradoxically, a policy originally designed to promote educational equity through increased choice and regional differentiation helped to create its opposite (OECD, 1998, p. 79). In Russia, decentralization was initiated, but local capacity was not sufficiently developed to take advantage of the new government's proposal.

Existence and quality of innovations/pressure groups – the limited reach of pedagogical reform

In Russia, the process of educational decentralization has brought about some interesting pedagogical innovations concentrated mainly in schools with established records of scholarship (i.e. gymnasia and lycées)[11] and those which have entered into partnerships with foreign schools and professional associations (OECD, 1998, p. 54). Currently, many of these schools are directed either by members of Dneprov's original reform group or by independent innovative thinkers. Among

10 For example, the law and subsequent decrees stipulated that education was to receive no less than 10 per cent of the GNP (it is currently at 8 per cent); that all students were to receive free full secondary education through grade 11 (this has been compromised by the introduction of tuition fees in private and selected state schools); that teachers' salaries would match those of government employees earning the equivalent of US$110 per month (the current salary for junior teachers is US$8/month; for senior teachers it is US$40/month (Kromov, 1999; Ignatov, 1999)). In 1995, the federal government honoured only about 67 per cent of its own education bill to the regions. As a result, it was necessary to carry over wage arrears into the following fiscal year (OECD, 1998, pp. 35–6).

11 Gymnasia and lycées are academic secondary schools that prepare students for university entrance.

these talented individuals are Alexander Naumovich Tubelsky (1999), president of the Association of Innovative Schools and Centres, and Director of the School of Self-Determination in Moscow; Alexi Borisovich Vorontsov (1999), director of the Moscow Association for Developmental Education[12] and principal of the Experimental Teaching Complex No. 1133 in Moscow; Anatoli Arkadievich Pinski (1999), director of the Association of Russian Schools, president of the Association of Moscow School Directors, and Director of School No. 1060 in Moscow; Alexandra Mihalovna Lenartovich (1999), principal of School No. 1321, 'Kovcheg', a unique 'integrated' special needs school in Moscow; Anatoli Georgievich Kasprjak (1999), principal of Moscow Pedagogical Gymnasium; and Evgeni Alexandrovich Yamburg (1999), principal of the elite Gymnasium No. 109 in Moscow.

The late 1980s saw the emergence of private consultants and experimental training groups which offered training alternatives based on the pedagogical models of these innovative schools (Kerr, 1991). One of the earliest was the aforementioned Eureka group, part of the innovative school movement which provided seminars and training sessions for teachers in Russia and the former USSR since 1990. Several other organizations, such as the Centre for Cultural Policy and the new Association for Developmental Education were also active in providing educational training opportunities. These – as well as many other local and private entrepreneurs – organized workshops for teachers, to facilitate the sharing and exchange of ideas and to offer training in new pedagogical paradigms, alternative teaching techniques, and imported models of education (based primarily on Montessori and Waldorf philosophies).

Although it is arguable that these organizations served as influential pressure groups for the transformation of Russian education, they too fell victim to a struggling economy. Dwindling enrolments forced some consultants either to dissolve or to extend into outlying regions and other countries in search of new clients.[13] In the final analysis, economic conditions compromised whatever initial

---

12 The Association for Developmental Education promotes Davydov's ideas concerning the use of Vygotskian psychology as a basis for classroom teaching (Davydov, 1995; Vorontsov, 1999). The model is conceptually sophisticated, but in most schools its implementation takes on a form not radically different from what transpires in a traditional classroom (Kerr, 1995). Davydov's model is more readily accepted by Russians because it originated in Russia (i.e. was not borrowed or adapted from Western pedagogy) and is based on the concept of 'social constructivism', popular in North America today. Developmental instruction has also garnered support from the Ministry of Education; since 1992 when Davydov and his colleagues began to disseminate the model in a well-elaborated and practical format, it has spread to more than 42 per cent of all Russian primary classrooms. The popularity of this model supports the truism that in educational reform small steps are easier for teachers to work with than major conceptual leaps that lack specifics (Kerr, 1996; Vorontsov, 1999).

13 Eureka even began offering summer programmes for pupils and teachers in England, the USA, and Cyprus. Many of these special workshops were regularly advertised through the pedagogical press (Kerr, 1995).

enthusiasm teachers exhibited for reform. When Tubelsky was asked what was happening to the innovators' movement – was it spreading and developing or had it died – he lamented, 'It hasn't died, but I think it's dying' (as cited in Kerr, 1995).

Fullan notes that the role of the community in the initiation process may take the form of 'exerting pressure for a solution to a problem, opposing a potential innovation or adoption, or doing nothing' (Fullan, 2001, p. 61). In Russia, it is clear that the innovators' movement was influential in pressing for educational change and in introducing teachers to new pedagogical models and offering them training opportunities to prepare for unfamiliar challenges. However, the influence of this movement has not reached the majority of teachers. Although there have been pockets of change and exciting innovative programmes, the majority of Russian classrooms have remained traditional; even, in Brodinsky's words (1992), 'as the winds of change sweep all around them' (p. 379).[14]

According to Pinski (1999), Russian parents are *not* perceived as a significant community pressure group. In an interview with the primary author, Pinksi explains: 'In the last decade of the innovative school movement, you will find brilliant pedagogical personalities: highly talented teachers, school directors and scientists. However, you will rarely find the voice of parents.' Although parental political activism and empowerment has been minimal, a new relationship between parents and schools *is* beginning to emerge. The first important step in this direction is the affirmation of the parents' rights to select the school they wish their children to attend, including the option of private schools. Parents of children with special needs are particularly active in school governance. For example, parents whose children attend Kovcheg School in Moscow recognize that both the regular school system and the segregated special-needs schools are harmful to children. In 1991, they founded a unique school in which 80 per cent of the student population is either deaf, has cerebral palsy, autism, epilepsy, developmental delays, asthma, behaviour problems or is classified as 'at-risk' for failure; 20 per cent have no special needs. A. M. Lenartovich, principal of Kovcheg School (which she describes as a 'thorn' in the side of society), has declined to register Kovcheg as a special needs school, in order to avoid the negative effects

---

14 Curricular innovation within the decentralization process involves providing teachers with greater choice of course materials. For example, there is now an opportunity to incorporate locally devised inputs into the school programme, which can help foster a sense of local identity and inform pupils about valuable aspects of their local heritage and institutions. Whereas the federal authorities prescribe a main core curriculum (60 per cent) that reflects the Russian national heritage, regions have the opportunity to contribute about 30 per cent of the curricular content, focusing on such regionally distinct areas as ethnicity, language, history, folklore, crafts, etc. Individual schools (which may want to extend programming in the English language, the arts, or the sciences) have control over the remaining 10 per cent (OECD, 1998, pp. 20, 88). The challenge is to preserve the overall unity of the various regions while simultaneously accommodating the great diversity of their peoples (OECD, 1998, p. 35).

of 'labelling'. Although not 'integrated' in the North American sense, this school is considered to be quite innovative (Lenartovich, 1999).

Fullan stresses the importance of parental involvement as a means of fostering a 'client orientation' for schools. As personal interactions between parents and schools expand and become institutionalized, greater trust and mutual engagement will begin to evolve. Parental involvement ensures that the school ultimately becomes responsive to the real needs of the community (Fullan, 1999, p. 46). This is precisely the type of relationship that is nurtured at Kovcheg School in Moscow.

Access to information – minimal knowledge-sharing among regions and municipalities

Fullan (2001) discusses 'access to information' in terms of teachers' contact with innovative ideas, which is essential to the success of any change effort. In Russia, 'access to information' may also refer to data about the evolving education system, which government requires in order to monitor the effects of current policy and make informed decisions about future reform. In the traditional USSR education system, the data that were gathered concerned quantitative characteristics, e.g. numbers of schools, students, teachers, graduates, school buildings, boarding facilities, etc. The current information base provides only limited data on the efficiency of schools, the quality of teaching, the cost effectiveness of the system, and the extent to which the design and delivery of new programmes meet changing market needs (OECD, 1998). Hindered by the current rigidity of the vertical administrative structure, 'knowledge sharing' among regions and municipalities is limited. In some cases, schools located in the same city *rayon* often must try to solve common problems independently. Clearly, more effective networking would benefit teachers and administrators who currently work in isolation, which would facilitate the development and adoption of the best educational programmes and teaching practices (OECD, 1998).

External change agents – Russia's ambivalent relationship with the West

Fullan classifies as external change agents those regional, state, or national bodies, external to the district, which stimulate or support change, particularly in the initiation phase (Fullan, 2001, p. 60). For purposes of this study, since the unit of analysis is the nation, external agents may be defined as those that impact the change process from outside the Russian Federation. There is evidence that substantial international activity is taking place in Russia at all levels of the education system from the highest administrative offices of government to the individual classroom. However, the overall impact of these external agents on the national direction of reform is less clear.

When Dneprov introduced the 1992 Law on Education, he realized that the goal of modernization required the integration of the Russian education system into the world community. Accordingly, the Law contained a provision regarding networking with international partners, such as the World Bank, the Carnegie Foundation, the United States International Agency (USIA), the British Council, and the Soros Foundation. Even prior to 1992, one of Dneprov's early initiatives as a Minister of Education was the establishment of ties with the Oslo-based International Movement Toward Educational Change (IMTEC), now known as the International Learning Cooperative on educational reform.[15]

The Soros Foundation has played a particularly significant role in Russia in the preparation of new *civics* courses and materials, including textbooks. Various international agencies have assisted with the development of university-level distance education programmes. For example, in Krasnoyarsk, the regional Centre for the Development of Education offers a number of courses jointly with the Open University in the United Kingdom (OECD, 1998, p. 75).[16] There has even been opportunity for international cooperation in the development of Russian education standards; in the Vologda region, for example, a Dutch-Russian testing centre was recently established. Using modern technology, the centre created and administered examinations for a range of school subjects and was responsible for collecting, analysing, and reporting student data to regional education officials. The centre has also organized a number of successful workshops for other regions interested in developing similar procedures (Kaliningrad, Stavropol, Saki) (OECD, 1998, p. 95). The British Council is also beginning to play an important role in educational reform in both central Russia (Moscow and St Petersburg) and remote areas of the Federation (e.g. Omsk, Krasnoyarsk, Volgograd, Tomsk, and Irkutsk). Projects range from curriculum development, educational management, and in-service training, to vocational education, special education for at-risk children, and the education rights of ethnic minorities (Lenskaya, 1999).[17] Specific British Council projects currently under way include: (a) At-Risk Children in the Nishny Novgorod Region, co-sponsored by Kibble Education and Care Centre, Scotland; (b) Developing Technology Education in the Nishny Novgorod region, co-sponsored by University of York in Northern Ireland; (c) Competency-Based Vocational Education and Training (a modular approach to teaching) in the Omsk region, co-sponsored by the Scottish Qualifications Authority in Glasgow; (d) Retraining Teachers in Civics Education in the Krasnoyarsk region, co-sponsored by the Citizenship Foundation in London, England; (e) In-Service Training for Educational Administrators in the Krasnoyarsk

15 In fact, it was Dneprov's openness to Western contacts during his tenure as Minister of Education that, some believe, contributed to the increased alienation of many of his original supporters, and ultimately to his resignation from office (Johnson, 1997).

16 Moscow's University of the Russian Academy of Education, the first private university to receive official state accreditation (in 1995) was initially modelled after the United Kingdom's Open University concept (Bim-Bad, 1999).

17 Each region was responsible for seeking out an international partner from the United Kingdom. It was only through the recent devolution of finances from the federal government that the regions have been able to initiate and fund such projects independently (Lenskaya, 1999).

region, co-sponsored by Kent Advisory Service in Kent County, Great Britain; (f) National Professional Qualification for Head Teachers in the Sochi region, co-sponsored by the Gloucestershire Education County Council; (g) English Language In-Service Training for Secondary School Teachers (KINSET Project) in the Krasnoyarsk region with participant outreach in Omsk, Sochi and Volgograd, sponsored by the British Council; and (h) English Language Examination Project (SPEX): Development of New School Leaving Examinations in English in St. Petersburg, sponsored by the British Council.

Russia's relationship with the West, however, remains ambivalent. Despite significant international activity in such areas as management, curriculum, training, assessment and distance education, the majority of individuals interviewed for the current study did not perceive these interventions as significantly having shaped the nature of the innovations that took place in this country. Although funding partners for projects have been actively pursued, there is tacit, if not obdurate resistance on the part of many Russian educators to the adoption of 'western-style' models of education.[18] Fullan (1999, p. 17) provides evidence that if knowledge is imposed rather than 'grown', it will fail. He adds, '... successful reforms in one place are partly a function of good ideas and largely a function of the conditions under which the ideas flourished. Successful innovations ... fail to be replicated because the wrong thing is being replicated – the reform itself, instead of the conditions which spawned its success' (p. 64).

Discussion

The objective of this chapter is not to provide an exhaustive analysis of the experience of change, but rather to explore the utility of Fullan's framework for helping us understand Russia's post-1991 initiation of change. The data clearly support the value of Fullan's framework. Education reform in Russia began before the dissolution of the Soviet Union, when it was clear that the education system was rapidly deteriorating. Fuelled by the spirit of *perestroika* and supported by the increasing presence and voice of the educational media, the innovative school movement, led by Dneprov, was born. Although Dneprov's 1992 Law on Education laid the groundwork for significant educational change in the Federation, bureaucratic counterforces seriously hindered its progress. Initial teacher support for change has more recently been compromised by devastating economic hardships. Teacher enthusiasm has given way to disillusionment, and public confidence in the government's ability to effect educational change has been shaken. Reform has been adversely affected by the absence of appropriate local administrative infrastructures to support the decentralization of administrative and

---

18 Innovative programmes, they argue, are inspired by internal sources – talented educators who recognize the need to challenge the traditional school system and to offer the youth of Russia an alternative for the twenty-first century.

fiscal responsibilities to regional educational authorities. While the new Law on Education (1992) enabled the emergence of a number of unique innovative programmes directed by talented and progressively minded school principals (Polyzoi *et al.*, 2002), many of these programmes became victims of the economic crisis. As a result, many principals were compelled to explore creative ways to survive, such as charging parents supplementary tuition fees for specialized courses (e.g. music, theatre, English language), renting out parts of their schools to generate extra revenue; encouraging parental involvement; offering yearly in-service teacher training; and marketing their own curricular materials (Lisovskaya and Karpov, 2001; Polyzoi *et al.*, 2002). Knowledge-sharing, as it relates to innovative school programmes among regions and municipalities, is still limited – hindered by the rigidity of the current education system's vertical administrative structure. In addition, although numerous international partnerships have developed between Western and Russian educational institutions, the impact of the West on the reforms taking shape in Russia remains unclear.

Although Fullan's schema is rich in detail and multivariate in approach, there are certain dynamics of the change process which it does not address. For example, in Russia, change has not typically proceeded in a linear fashion; it has been much more an integrative and organic process. As Bîrzea (1994) elaborates, systems in transition, such as many post-Soviet countries, are initially characterized by the coexistence of old and new structures. The greater the differences between a system's initial and final states (i.e. the less common or overlapping elements they share), the more difficult the transition process will be; if the two states are highly disparate, chaos will result. In order to facilitate change, a 'bridge' or intermediate state must be constructed with common features spanning the old and the new (Venda, 1991, 1999). This is evident in the Russian experience. As Russia struggles to move from a highly centralized, teacher-directed education system to a liberal, democratic, and child-centred curriculum, educators are searching for a more widely acceptable centrist position (Kerr, 1996). The window of opportunity for dramatic change, which opened immediately following the collapse of the Union, is slowly closing. Change is now more measured and cautious, as the reform movement's recent tendency towards retrenchment – perhaps in an attempt to bridge the 'revolutionary leap' initiated by Dneprov in his 1992 Law on Education – attests.[19]

As well as not fully capturing the organic nature of large-scale reform in politically, socially, and economically volatile settings, Fullan's framework does not

19 The federal government's recent attempt to introduce national educational 'standards' provides some evidence for the existence of this tendency. Conservative elements (some of whom *started* as members of the reform movement), now argue for the importance of standards as a means of preserving a 'unified educational space' within Russia and preventing further fragmentation in the Federation. Members of the reform movement, however, see this as a regressive measure, i.e. as a 'cover' for strengthening the centrist position at a time when the regions need more flexibility and freedom, not less (Dneprov, 1999).

fully account for the unique preconditions that precipitated large-scale change in post-Soviet countries, i.e. it does not acknowledge the importance of the stage-setting that allowed the initiation of major national reform to proceed with such speed and breadth. Bîrzea (1995) incorporates these characteristic preconditions in his four-phase model of educational transformation: *deconstruction, stabilization, reconstruction* and *counter-reform*. The first two of these stages may be understood as preceding Fullan's 'initiation' stage. In the USSR, the *deconstruction period* was initiated by Gorbachev during the era of *perestroika*. It was at this time that the first steps towards dismantling the Russian education system were taken. Once the Marxist-Leninist ideology had been discredited, schools had little choice but to deconstruct their outdated ideology-driven education system. Curricular innovations first proposed by the Soviet ministry in 1988 were extended in the early 1990s. Indeed, Russia's attempt to *stabilize* these reforms began with the introduction of the Law on Education in 1992. Although this law provided an important framework for educational transformation, attempts to move forward with substantive educational *reconstruction* have been hindered by a number of other factors, to which Bîrzea (1995) alludes. According to Bîrzea (1995), change in post-Communist countries is dependent on reform in other domains: *economic, ideological,* and *political.* Dneprov (1999a) supports Bîrzea's views. He elaborates: 'Russian educational reform has been unable to break through the economic barriers which have increasingly paralysed the education system. The ideological breaking away has in some ways been even more problematic because it addresses the values, attitudes and mentalities of the Russian people. Pedagogical models that emphasize conformity, the collective, and centralized control are inconsistent with those that emphasize individual choice, self-development, and independent thinking. In addition, reform in Russia is aggravated by the political context, in particular the recent attempt by the various communist factions within the Duma to fuel the fires of opposition, to repeatedly impeach President Yeltsin, to resurrect the nostalgic past by rekindling feelings of nationalism.' This is what Bîrzea (1995) refers to as the *counter-reform stage* – the emergence of residual communism that serves to block or slow down the pace of educational reform.[20]

Is the process of educational reform that was initiated in Russia in 1990 continuing to evolve? Our response is a qualified 'yes' (see also Dneprov, 1999b). Although educational reform as a conscious targeted political action by government was concluded in 1992 with the passage of the Law on Education, the educational reform movement as a large-scale spontaneous process of internal change is continuing to gain strength in Russia. Situated amidst oppressive economic conditions and obstructive conservative political forces, Russian educa-

---

20 Bîrzea (1995) reminds us that it is a paradox of democracy in the context of an underdeveloped political culture that democratic processes may serve neo-communist factions and undermine the very reform that embodies the democratic principles.

tion has shown a measure of resiliency and resolve. Despite devastating economic hardships and waning political involvement (complicated by quasi-reformists and regressive political tendencies), an emergent progressive education movement in Russia is finally beginning to move forward, albeit with difficulty. This is due largely to the efforts of a motivated, inspired pedagogical community, innovative teachers and administrators, and committed regional directors throughout the Federation.

Although Fullan's conceptual framework does not directly address the revolutionary nature of change and is comparatively linear in its approach, Bîrzea's schema provides a dynamic overlay more consistent with an organic picture of the Russian change process. The two models or frameworks of change complement one another; when applied together, they provide a clearer understanding of the transition process in the former Communist countries in Eastern and Central Europe. What emerges from the application of both these schemas is a dynamic, interactive picture of change – one that is much more complex and multivariate than either model could offer alone. As we learn more about rapid and dramatic change in Russia, as we discover what forces are relevant in successful reform, and as we appreciate the complexity of a dynamic, living, and continuously evolving system, we are in a better position to direct and shape change in positive ways. Although (given our current knowledge of educational change theory) harnessing these forces may be difficult, this study represents the beginning of a framework for thinking about change, particularly in nations undergoing dramatic and sudden transformation.

References

Anweiler, O. (1992) Some historical aspects of educational change in the former Soviet Union and Eastern Europe. In D. Phillips and M. Kaser, M. (Eds), *Education and Economic Change in Eastern Europe and the Former Soviet Union* (Series: *Oxford Studies in Comparative Education*) (pp. 29–39). Wallingford, Oxfordshire: Triangle Books.

Bim-Bad, B.M. (1999) Interview by the primary author, Moscow, March 22, 1999.

Bîrzea, C. (1994) *Educational Policies of the Countries in Transition*. Strasbourg: Council of Europe Press.

Bîrzea, C. (1995, September) Educational reform and educational research in Central-Eastern Europe: The case of Romania. Paper presented at the IBE International Meeting on Educational Reform and Educational Research, Tokyo, Japan.

Bolotov, V.A. (1995) The reform of education in New Russia: a background report for the OECD. Moscow: unpublished, Retrieved November 21, 1999 from <http://www.indiana.edu/~isre/NEWSLETTER/vol6no2/OECD.htm>

Brodinsky, B. (1992) The impact of perestroika on Soviet education. *Phi Delta Kappan*, **73**(5), 378–385.

Davydov, V.V. (1995) The influence of L.S. Vygotsky on education, theory, research, and practice. *Educational Researcher*, **24**(3), 12–21.

Dimova, I. (1999) Interview by the primary author, Moscow, April 5, 1999.

Dneprov, E. (1999a) Interview by the primary author, Moscow, March 25, 1999.

Dneprov, E. (1999b) *Three Sources and Three Components of the Current School Crisis*. Moscow: University of the Russian Academy of Education [in Russian].

Elkof, B. (1997) From the editor: The state of Russian education. *ISRE Virtual Newsletter*, 6(1). Retrieved October 26, 1999 from <http://www.indiana.edu/~isre/NEWSLETTER/vol6no1/editorial.htm>

Fullan, M. (1993) *Change Forces: Probing the Depths of Educational Reform*. London: The Falmer Press.

Fullan, M. (1999) *Change Forces: The Sequel*. London: The Falmer Press.

Fullan, M. (2001) *The New Meaning of Educational Change* (3rd edn). New York: Teachers College Press.

Ignatov, A.M. (1999) Interview by the primary author, Moscow, March 18, 1999.

Izvestia (1988, December 24). p. 3.

Johnson, M.S. (1997) Visionary hopes and technocratic fallacies in Russian education. *Comparative and International Education Society*, 41(2), 219–225.

Kasprjak, A.G. (1999) Interview by the primary author, Moscow, April 6, 1999.

Kerr, S.T. (1990) Will glasnost lead to perestroika? Directions of educational reform in the USSR. *Educational Researcher*, 19(7), 26–31.

Kerr, S.T. (1991) Beyond dogma: teacher education in the USSR. *Journal of Teacher Education*, 42(5), 332–349.

Kerr, S.T. (1995, October) Teachers' continuing education and Russian school reform. Paper presented at the Conference of the American Association for the Advancement of Slavic Studies, Washington, DC. Retrieved October 20, 1999, from <http://weber.uwashington.edu/~stkerr/concrut.htm>

Kerr, S.T. (1996) *The Re-centering of Russian Education*. Comments as part of a roundtable at the American Association for the Advancement of Slavic Studies, Boston. Retrieved November 17, 1999, from <http://weber.u.washington.edu/~stkerr/aaass.html>

Kerr, S.T. (1998) The new Russian education reform: back to the future? *ISRE Virtual Newsletter*, 7(1), 1–6. Retrieved November 30, 1999, from <http://www.indiana.edu/~isre/NEWSLETTER/vol7no1/Kerr.htm>

Kromov, K.M. (1999) Interview by the primary author, Moscow, March 18, 1999.

Krugliakov, V.M. (1999) Interview by the primary author, Moscow, March 23, 1999.

Lenartovich, A.M. (1999) Interview by the primary author, Moscow, April 8, 1999.

Lenskaya, L. (1999) Interview by the primary author, Moscow, March 26, 1999.

Lisovskaya, E. and Karpov, V. (2001) The perplexed world of Russian private schools: findings from field research. *Comparative Education*, 37(1), 43–64.

Mays, A., Polyzoi, E. and Gardner, S. (1997) The Czech Experience of the initiation of educational change since 1989: is a North American model applicable? *Canadian and International Education*, 26(1), 32–53.

Nechaev, N.N. (1999) Interview by the primary author, Moscow, March 25, 1999.

OECD (1998) *Reviews of National Policies for Education: Russian Education*. Paris, France: Organization for Economic Co-operation and Development (OECD).

Pinski, A.A. (1999) Interview by the primary author, Moscow, March 30, 1999.

Polyzoi, E., Nazarenko, T. and Anchan, J. (2002, March) *A comparative analysis of four innovative schools in Russia: understanding the process of educational reform*. Paper presented at the annual meeting of the Comparative and International Education Society, Orlando, Florida.

Rust, V.D. (1992) An interview with Edward Dneprov: school reform in the Russian Republic. *Phi Delta Kappan*, **73**(5), 375–377.

Rust, V.D., Knost, P. and Wichmann, J. (1994) Education and youth in Central and Eastern Europe: a comparative assessment. In V.D. Rust, P. Knost, and J. Wichmann (Eds), *Education and the Values Crisis in Central and Eastern Europe* (pp. 281–308). Frankfurt, Germany: Peter Lang.

Tubelsky, A.N. (1999) Interview by the primary author, Moscow, April 1, 1999.

Vaillant, J. (1997) *A provocative report: the reform of education in new Russia: a background report for the OECD (Review of Government Report)*. Retrieved November 3, 1999, from <http://www.indiana.edu/~isre/NEWSLETTER/vol6no 1/OECDreview.htm>

Venda, V. (1991) Transformation dynamics in complex systems. *Journal of the Washington Academy of Sciences*, **81**(4), 163–184.

Venda, V. (1999) Interview by the primary author, Winnipeg, Manitoba, Canada, May 5, 1999.

Vorontsov, A.B. (1999) Interview by the primary author, Moscow, March 26, 1999.

Yamburg, E.A. (1999) Interview by the primary author, Moscow, April 6, 1999.

3

FORCES AFFECTING THE IMPLEMENTATION OF EDUCATIONAL CHANGE IN THE CZECH REPUBLIC

A dynamic model[1]

Eleoussa Polyzoi, University of Winnipeg, Manitoba, Canada
Marie Černá, Charles University, Prague, the Czech Republic

Introduction

'Few events in recent history have been as sudden or as dramatic as the collapse of Communism and the adoption of parliamentary democracy in those nations formerly under the control of the Soviet Union' (Beresford-Hill, 1998, p. 9). While the political reorientation of these nations and the development of a market economy are of immediate concern, the importance of educational change in the country's long-term rebuilding processes must be acknowledged. Because this transformation has taken place in Central Europe within a remarkably short period of time, the Czech experience provides a unique opportunity – a 'living laboratory' – for the investigation of educational change.

At least three features of the Czech case set it apart from the Russian (described in the preceding chapter). First, the initiation of educational change in the Czech Republic occurred almost literally overnight; in Russia, reform was initiated several years *before* the 1991 collapse of the Soviet Union and continues to the present time, under tumultuous circumstances. Second, in the Czech Republic, change for the most part took place in the absence of any established plan for achieving a desired vision or goal: the concept of 'planning' – firmly associated with the Communist regime – was collectively rejected after the 'Velvet Revolution'. In Rus-

---

1 This chapter is an adaptation of an article that appeared in *Comparative Education Review*, February 2001, **45**(1), 64–84. Reprint permission granted © 2001 by the Comparative and International Education Society, The University of Chicago Press.

sia, by contrast, change (at least initially) was characterized by a clear vision, its implementation, however, was obstructed by deteriorating economic conditions. Third, in the Czech Republic, Communism was *imposed externally* by the Soviet Union after World War II, whereas in Russia, communist ideology emerged from *within*, born of the 1917 Bolshevik Revolution (Dneprov, 1999).

This chapter represents the second phase of a larger exploratory study that examines the Czech experience within the context of a framework of educational change proposed by Michael Fullan (1993, 1999, 2001). While the first phase examined the *initiation* of change as observed in the events immediately following the Velvet Revolution (Mays *et al.*, 1997), Phase 2 examines the *implementation* stage of the Czech experience: the extent to which the system was transformed and the degree to which changes endured or failed to survive beyond the initiation stage in the two to three years following 1989. We argue that Fullan's conceptual framework, informed primarily by North American examples, does have value for illuminating the events in the Czech Republic; however, we propose a revised framework which better accounts for the dynamic character of dramatic and sudden change typical of former Soviet-satellite countries.

Czechoslovakia under Communist rule

Following World War II, the Czech Republic entered a long period of Communist rule (1948–1989). Marxism-Leninism became the dominant ideology of the education system. A rigid, centralized administrative structure was introduced, with a monolithic, federally controlled curriculum which left little room for individual pedagogical initiatives. Textbooks were provided by the state, and educational needs were guided by a centralized human-power-planning strategy. Conformity was enforced, and access to higher education was based on Communist Party membership (Ministry of Education, Youth and Sports of the Czech Republic, 1994). In 1968, Communist Party secretary Alexander Dubcek sought to implement 'socialism with a human face', reforming the country's economy and easing political oppression during the 'Prague Spring'. Unhappy with these developments, Soviet authorities invaded Czechoslovakia and suppressed Dubcek's counter-revolution. What followed was 21 years of an even more repressive system under the leadership of Gustav Husak (Pilátová, 1995).

In autumn 1989, after the fall of Communism in Hungary and Poland and the fall of the Berlin Wall, the 'Velvet Revolution' began in Czechoslovakia. Despite crackdowns, Czechs increasingly staged demonstrations and massive strikes in Prague and other major cities. By November of that year, the Communist government resigned and Vaclav Havel, the long-imprisoned playwright, became the Czech Republic's new president. These events prompted a series of changes in the nation's political, economic, and education systems. The Czech constitution was modified to eliminate Communist Party influence and to remove Marxist-Leninist ideology from the dominant position it held in all sectors of society. A pluralistic parliamentary system was reinstated; the centrally planned, rigidly controlled economy was replaced with a free-market economy within a democratic framework, and privatization of formerly state-run enterprises was permitted along with foreign-capital investment and free-market price competition (Průcha and Walterová, 1992). These events precipitated a major contradiction of values within Czech political and economic structures. The new principles expressed in legislation prompted the initiation of major changes in education as well.

Fullan's conceptual framework

According to Fullan, most researchers acknowledge three broad stages to the process of educational change: *initiation*, *implementation*, and *institutionalization* (see Part I of this book). While the preceding chapter on Russian education focuses on the 'initiation' of change (the first stage in the change process), the current examination focuses on 'implementation', the second stage. Whereas initiation consists of the process that leads up to change and includes a decision to adopt or proceed with it, implementation involves the first attempts to put an idea or reform into practice. By contrast, 'institutionalization' refers to whether the change gets built in as an ongoing part of the system or disappears by way of a decision to discard it or through attrition (Fullan, 2001, p. 69).

The implementation of change

Fullan organizes the factors which affect implementation into three main categories:

1 The specific nature of the innovation or change project: Does it address a significant need? Are the objectives clear? What is the level of difficulty and extent of change required?
2 External factors which press for and facilitate change: What role do political groups, reform organizations, government bureaucracies, and the community play in enabling change to take place?
3 Local characteristics which affect the degree to which the innovation is supported by its direct participants or stakeholders: To what extent do the teachers, parents, students, etc. support change?[2]

---

2 The degree to which these factors influence implementation depends on various dynamic forces that provide a vivid, interactive picture of the change process. These forces or themes include the following: What type of leadership has characterized the change process? Are plans flexible and continuously adjusted to take advantage of unexpected developments? Is a collaborative work culture encouraged so as to extend involvement of all participants? Is staff development or resource assistance provided throughout the implementation stage? Is the change process continually monitored, and have effective coping strategies been developed to deal with emergent problems? Have structural changes (changes in administration, governance, finance, policies, physical space, etc.) been made to accommodate the successful implementation of the programme?

Method/data sources

Between March and June of 1997, the authors conducted lengthy interviews in Prague with over 30 key individuals, including members of the Ministry of Education, teacher educators, university researchers, members of advocacy and school reform organizations, teachers, school administrators, parents, and students; interviewees were selected because of the central role they played in the transformation of the education system. A wide variety of participants was deliberately chosen in accordance with Fullan's concept of 'shared meaning of change' (2001, p. 9). A number of interviewees also provided important primary documents related to the change process of educational transformation, as a supplement to the interviews. These documents described selected innovative programmes, provided statistical data on various aspects of the education system, and described legislative changes that have been introduced in the Czech Republic since 1989. The authors also had an opportunity to informally observe selected classrooms at both the primary and secondary levels, in both state and private institutions for cognitively challenged children and youth.

The authors acknowledge that their research was confined to a limited geographical area (Prague) and involved a limited number of interviewees. As well, it is inevitable that the authors' interpretations reflect their own perspectives, which of necessity are informed both by those of their interlocutor and by the historical moment at which the interviews took place. This proviso notwithstanding, the authors' investigations garnered a wealth of primary information. Data was collected from individuals who played a key role in the Czech Republic's initial transition period, including members of the Prague reform movement.

The interviews were based upon an unstructured questionnaire. Questions were open-ended; as the interview unfolded, the researchers elicited further information by posing additional probe questions. The following questions served as a guide for the interviews.

1 How have the political, economic, and social changes that have taken place in the Czech Republic since 1991 impacted on the education system?
2 What factors prompted the onset of these changes?
3 Is there a vision that characterizes these changes?
4 Who are the educational decision and policy makers?
5 Are parents empowered to make decisions in schools?
6 Who are the key individuals/organizations/government bodies that have pushed for/initiated/supported change?
7 What problems have you encountered in the transformation of the Czech education system?
8 What have been the barriers and facilitators of change?
9 What does the future hold for Czech education? Elaborate.

These questions were overlaid with probes which helped clarify:

1   the perceived need for and clarity of educational change;
2   the influence of the past – the role of pre-revolutionary models of education;
3   the heritage of the communist regime and the importance of 'reculturing' (see Fullan, 1998);
4   the reciprocal relationship between cultural (norms, habits, skills, beliefs) and structural change (physical environment, organizational arrangements, finance, governance, curriculum, training, etc.);
5   the complexity of the change that is required;
6   external factors that press for and advance change;
7   the influence of the West in facilitating change;
8   the role of reform organizations; and
9   the degree to which change is supported by its direct participants: teachers, parents, administrators, students, business community, churches, private schools, etc.

Interviews were approximately one to two hours long; about 50 hours of interview material were recorded on audiocassettes. Slightly over half of the interviews were conducted in English. The second author of this chapter, as well as a linguistic student and a journalism student from Charles University, Prague, alternated as interpreters in those cases where the interviewees spoke only Czech. Analyses of the data took the form of examining the transcriptions of the interviews and the extensive notes and documents acquired by the researchers. They were then matched against the model and elements of *implementation* of change as identified by Fullan in order to understand transformation as a 'change' process.

The case: an analysis of the implementation of educational change

Fullan's framework for understanding educational change speaks most directly to change and innovation at the level of classrooms, schools or school districts, although it does *not* exclude change at the national level (Fullan, 2000, 2001). In the case of the Czech Republic, it could be argued that educational change was not simply a matter of an innovation or project being introduced at some local level. The unit of analysis for educational transformation in the Czech Republic, at least in the case of the original impetus for change, was the nation. The current analysis, therefore, will focus on the implementation of change at this broader level.

The 'Velvet Revolution' was followed by immediate national consensus that change, after 40 years of Communist rule, was desirable. This period, which lasted 2–3 years, has been characterized as one of euphoria, of great expectations, and of an unwavering commitment to change (Kalous, 1997; Kotásek, 1997). In the several months following November 1989, the most salient characteristics of the totalitarian system were rapidly eliminated (Průcha and Walterová, 1992; Mays *et al.*, 1997; Rýdl, 1997).

1   The Marxist doctrine was abolished from primary, secondary and university school curricula – a move which inadvertently created a vacuum of instructional materials for use in history, social science, and civic studies.
2   Decentralization of the school system was initiated, giving more responsibility to teachers, principals, and local authorities; institutions of higher education were accorded autonomy and political independence.
3   The removal of the compulsory status of Russian as a foreign language resulted in English becoming the foreign language of choice among students.
4   New legislation permitted the creation of private and religious schools; this led to a shift from a needs-based to a normative system of school funding in which money followed the student. Since students were free to select the school they would attend, schools became very competitive, developing alternative curricula and unique programmes to attract more students.

While these initial legislative changes took place fairly quickly, the implementation of more systemic structural, curricular, and administrative changes in the Czech education system posed a greater challenge.

The specific nature of the innovation

Perceived need for and clarity of change

For change to be successful, the general populace must perceive a need for change; what is more, the steps in the change process must be clear. Fullan (2001, p. 75) notes that innovations are often attempted without a careful examination of a need for change. Recognition of a need is an important 'readiness' factor associated with subsequent implementation of change. The people involved must perceive both that the needs being addressed are significant and that at least some progress is being made toward meeting them.

In the months following the 'Velvet Revolution', the ensuing administrative and ideological power vacuum in the Czech Republic created a sense of urgency for change. Although the public joined in the call for legislative reform, there was no consensus about the direction such change should take or how to navigate through the difficult terrain ahead. Some were in favour of permitting the free market to decide the direction of educational change; others advocated a slower, more cautious approach, allowing time for the development of a vision (Kalous, 1997; Mays *et al.*, 1997). While Fullan agrees that vision is necessary for success, he cautions that reflective experience is needed before a plausible vision can be formed. 'Vision emerges from, more than it precedes, action. Even then, it is always provisional ... Visions coming later, does not mean that they are not worked on ... They are pursued more authentically while avoiding premature formalization' (Fullan, 1993, p. 28).

The influence of the past – the challenge of 'reculturing' the Czech education system

Jaroslav Kalous, director of the Institute for the Development of Education at Charles University in Prague, addresses the 'inertia of acquired attitudes and behaviour patterns' – a legacy of the Communist regime – which he believes is the most significant, yet elusive, barrier to educational reform in the Czech Republic (Kalous, 1997). By 'attitudes and behaviour patterns' Kalous means work habits that are deeply rooted in the past, such as acting only according to detailed instructions 'from above' (i.e. following centrally prescribed curricula), or using outdated teaching methods and content (i.e. an authoritarian, teacher-centred method of instruction, and encyclopaedic curricular content). Cesar Bîrzea, director of the Institute of Education Sciences in Bucharest, explains that a paradoxical coexistence of old and new structures is typical of states in transition (Bîrzea, 1994). The Czech Republic is no exception.

Fullan defines 'reculturing' as a process of redoing and rethinking, of unlearning and relearning (Fullan, 1998). The events in the Czech Republic immediately following the revolution led to a contradiction between the new principles of democracy, humanism, and liberalism and the old, rigid, highly bureaucratic educational structure. Evidence of this contradiction can be found in the centralization tendencies of schools in despite of the proclaimed general principle of decentralization (Rýdl, 1997). The newly created District School Offices are a case in point.[3] Under the former system, education was governed by a number of district and regional committees under the authority of the Ministry of the Interior and the Communist Party. Following the dissolution of these committees after 1989, new school offices were set up in each district to ensure links between the Minister of Education and the individual municipalities. These offices were directly responsible to the Ministry of Education. Although, in a number of cases, the school offices were instrumental in introducing innovative programmes and methods at the local school level, the great majority have remained mere del-

---

3 The Czech Republic is divided into 86 districts. School Offices were not only developed in each district, district school councils were also established in each municipality to support municipality interests within each district. In 1993, the Minister of Education also allowed schools to establish school boards with parent representation. Currently, there is no regional administrative unit (there are 10 regions in the Czech Republic) to deal with educational matters. The absence of any other unit between the School Office at the lower level and the Ministry of Education at the higher level is perceived as a weakness in the vertical administrative structure of the education system (Kalous, 1997).

egates of the central ministry, thus recreating the very administrative structure they were designed to replace.[4]

Fullan indicates that a reciprocal relationship exists between cultural change (norms, habits, skills, beliefs) and structural change (physical environment, organizational arrangements, roles, finance, governance, curriculum, training, etc.). He clarifies: 'this relationship is much more powerful when teachers and administrators begin working in new ways only to discover that school structures are ill-fitted to the new orientations and must be altered. This is a more productive sequence than the reverse when rapidly implemented new structures create confusion, ambiguity, and conflict ultimately leading to retrenchment' (Fullan, 1993, p. 68).

In the case of the Czech Republic, the relationship between cultural and structural change was not static or linear. This was reflected not only in the Ministry's attempt to decentralize the education system but also in the new role of the school inspectorate. In the past, the school inspectorate had been an important ideological and political tool for the totalitarian regime's control over schools; over the years, it had steadily grown to a staff of approximately 1,200 central, regional, and local inspectors in the Czech Republic. However, after 1989, the entire inspectorate body was dismissed, and experienced teachers were invited to compete for school-inspector positions. The old structure of the inspectorate was out of step with its new mandate; as a result, it is currently undergoing fundamental changes, both in its function and goals as well as in its method of carrying out responsibilities. With the greater autonomy now enjoyed by schools, it is likely that the inspectorate will shift from being controlling and repressive to being more supportive and consultative (Kalous, 1997).

The complexity of change – a focus on the curriculum

According to Fullan (2001), 'complexity' refers to the difficulty and extent of the change required of those individuals responsible for implementation. He adds, 'While complexity creates problems for implementation, it may result in greater change because more is attempted. On the other hand, while complex change promises to accomplish more, it also demands more effort, and failure takes a

---

4   This tacit tendency to maintain central control, despite the attempt to move towards decentralization, is less evident at the school level. After 1989, schools gained greater autonomy: they gained the freedom to manage their own budgets as well as considerable freedom on matters relating to staff, administration, and, to a certain degree, pedagogy. Directors were made responsible not only for the quality and effectiveness of the teaching process but also (gradually) for the financial management of the school, for appointing and dismissing teachers, and for relations with the municipality and public. All state-administered secondary schools gained the status of legal entities, and all private and denominational schools became entirely independent organizations. The status of 'legal entity' is also being gradually extended to basic schools and other state-administered educational establishments.

greater toll' (2001, p. 78). There is no doubt that change in the Czech Republic was massive, multi-level, and highly complex. It involved the governance and administration of the school system, the curriculum at all levels of education, the evaluation and assessment of programmes, the re-allocation of financial resources, and the development of pre-service and in-service teacher training.

Currently, reform plans in the Czech Republic are in many ways in their formative stages.[5] According to a recent report of the Organization for Economic Cooperation and Development (OECD), the change initiatives are entering unevenly into pedagogical practice and are encountering some resistance from teachers, for example, in the form of a fragmented understanding of different elements of the curriculum (goals, content, process, and evaluation); a reliance on the central curricular model and an unwillingness to take risks or to assume individual responsibility; a concentration on the encyclopaedic aspect of teaching without linking it to acquisition of skills, competence, and practice; and a preference for traditional authoritarian teacher-student relations (OECD, 1996).

A number of interviewees also expressed concern that the Ministry of Education's curricular reform had been developed in 'top down' fashion, without adequate consultation with other teachers, academics, and pedagogical experts. The Czech Parliament is responsible for drafting education laws but there is no nominated body of consultants at the Ministry of Education who can serve as advisors to Parliament. The initiative for changes in legislation comes exclusively from the Minister of Education (Kotásek, 1997). The OECD, in a recent review of the education system in the Czech Republic, proposed the creation of the National Curriculum Council to address this vacuum (Kotásek, 1997). The absence of a collaborative framework has been identified as a significant barrier to implementation of educational reform (Kovařovic, 1997). Without such a framework, ownership and commitment to changes among those directly affected becomes more problematic. A culture of consultation is just beginning to develop within the infrastructure of the current educational system.

According to Fullan, consultation is critical for any successful change, but it must be facilitated both from inside and from outside a system. Differences must not be avoided, but rather incorporated in problem solving; this approach is associated with creative breakthroughs – particularly under complex, turbulent conditions (Fullan, 1999, p. 22). Fullan elaborates, 'Put another way, the two-way street of "inside-outside" is a far more powerful metaphor than top-down-bottom-up thinking ... It places internal collaboration (at the school,

---

5 As an incentive for change, state requirements have been relaxed, permitting all state school directors the right to adjust up to 10 per cent of the standard curriculum and up to 30 per cent of the content of individual subjects (Kašová, 1997). The 1995 amendment to the Education Act allowed for the existence of alternative options for national curricula, other than those in place prior to 1989. The Ministry also permitted schools to propose alternative 'experimental' curricula, subject to approval (Kalous, 1997).

divisional levels), and external collaboration (at the state or national levels) as a high priority for success ... Effective organizations couple their internal problem-solving capacities with constant access to and consideration of external knowledge' (Fullan, 1999, p. 43).

The scope of the proposed educational reform in the Czech Republic was extensive, and while the need for change was nationally recognized, some reluctance and even inertia was evident in the system. A clear vision to guide the change process was absent; a culture of consultation had not yet had time to develop, and the educational heritage of the Communist regime – both structural and cultural – could not be easily discarded. The task of reshaping the education system remained a veritable challenge.

External factors which press for and facilitate change

Fullan, in his discussion of change and reform, primarily considers classrooms, schools, and districts as units of analysis. While this is suitable for an examination of change at the local level, a broader perspective is necessary when analyzing educational transformation and external factors influencing change in a post-Soviet nation. Global economic and political forces, which helped bring about the fall of Communism and the removal of Soviet hegemony over Eastern and Central Europe, provided the initial external impetus for change in the Czech Republic and the subsequent opportunity for influence by foreign agencies.

Global forces: the increasing influence of the West

It may be argued that, after the 'Velvet Revolution', foreign advisors and outside models of education played an important role in the initiation and implementation of reforms in the Czech Republic (Mays et al., 1997). For example, after 1989, Western organizations such as PHARE (European Union Program); the Soros Foundation; the British Council; the American Information Agency; Man, Education and New Technologies (MENT); Education for Democracy; and the Peace Corps provided increased funding for educational projects (Rýdl, 1997). There were also greater opportunities for teacher exchanges abroad, as well as for conferences and professional development with the potential to affect change or transformation at the classroom level. Finally, scholarly literature from around the world became more accessible to academics, policy makers, and educational researchers who, in turn, had the opportunity to work for change through the development of reform proposals. However, of all the external agencies, OECD was the most instrumental in providing the first strategic approach for comprehensive educational change (Kotásek, 1997). Its 1992 *Review on Higher Education in the Czech and Slovak Federal Republics* (OECD, 1992) has had a great impact on the development of policies relating to Czech higher education. The 1995 visit by the OECD review team resulted in the *Review of National Policies for Education: Czech Republic*, a critical document that helped provide concrete directives for changing the national educational system as a whole (OECD, 1996; Kalous, 1997).

The diminished role of national reform organizations

Soon after the Velvet Revolution, reform groups in the Czech Republic began to argue for the introduction of autonomous schools, a child-centred curriculum, the humanization of education, a focus on development of critical skills and problem solving, and diversification of curricular options. The three reform groups whose proposals were most influential were the Independent Interdisciplinary Group for the Reform of Education and School (NEMES), an independent, interdisciplinary group with several hundred members including teachers, psychologists, sociologists and economists; IDEA (Independent and Diverse Educational Alternatives), a group of mathematics educators; and Engaged/Involved Teachers Association (PAU), a group of approximately 300 reform-oriented teachers. In some cases, proposals were shelved and ignored; in other cases, selected ideas were incorporated into concrete reform proposals (Hausenblaus, 1997; Nováčková, 1997; Rýdl, 1997). The Ministry of Education saw experts from the academic community as often detached from political reality. Educational researchers, on the other hand, believed that policy makers had inadequate understanding of the requirements of a scientifically based analysis (OECD, 1996). While there may be some truth to both arguments, what cannot be disputed is that the role of the reform groups has perceptibly diminished in recent years. The window of opportunity for introducing change – initially wide open – has narrowed significantly, and the influence of reform organizations has correspondingly declined (Kalous, 1997; Nováčková, 1997; Hausenblaus, 1997; Kovařovic, 1997; Rýdl, 1997).

The government bureaucracy – the absence of a conceptually coherent policy

Educational issues have occupied a relatively small place in the election platforms of both Czech coalition and opposition parties, and are only addressed in very general terms. Political programmes seldom include concrete proposals for reform. This does not mean that Czech political parties have resisted reform, but simply that they have not been its real initiators (OECD, 1996). The role of Parliament is critical in that it must approve (although not necessarily initiate) every major reform. Between 1990 and 1992, the Ministry of Education approved and financially supported numerous experimental programmes in state, private, and church schools.[6] Currently, however, the process of educational reform is slowing

---

6 No database exists on the impact private schools have had on educational change. However, following the legislative approval of private schools in 1992, the expectation was that they would

down considerably. Fullan refers to this phenomenon as the 'implementation dip' (Fullan, 1998). The 'fall' is both psychological (where excitement about the innovation drops) and technical (where participants in the change process realize they need time to develop requisite skills). Fullan explains that a 'certain sense of failure accompanying success' is endemic to change.

A number of interviewees also pointed out the absence of long-term planning in the new educational-policy measures. Two brief examples merit some attention. In 1995, an amendment was introduced to the Education Act, requiring all students to complete nine years of education in the basic school (grades one to nine) before applying for admission to secondary school (grades ten to twelve). Formerly, students became eligible after eight grades of basic school and then could move to an upper secondary school in their ninth year. The unintended consequence of this legislation was a dramatic decrease in student population in the first year of secondary school (because students remained in basic school to complete grade nine). This resulted in reduced classes, the need to transfer some secondary teachers to basic schools, and in some cases dismissal of teachers due to insufficient enrolments (Kalous, 1997; Kotásek, 1997). In order to accommodate grade nine students, it was necessary to 'spread out' the basic school curriculum content by moving some lower level subjects to higher grades (Gregor, 1997). Another example of the Ministry of Education's lack of planning is the total dismantling of the in-service teacher training institutes because of their use under the old regime as an instrument of indoctrination. In 1989, the Ministry summarily dismissed approximately 600 teacher trainers, only to discover that they were left with no mechanism for training current teachers. Schools now receive funds to 'purchase' their own teacher-training services from ministry-accredited pedagogical centres and other organizations (Kalous, 1997). This lack of planning is not atypical of systems in transition: as Fullan (1999, p. 54) explains, 'The impatient search to address urgent problems makes the [education] system susceptible to ... superficial solutions.' Between 1992 and 1994, conflict developed between Parliament's Education, Science and Culture Committee, and the Ministry of Education. Noting the absence of a conceptually coherent programme, Parliament repeatedly asked the Minister to present a comprehensive educational policy for the country. Repeatedly, Parliament rejected the reports submitted by the minister (OECD, 1996).

serve as a catalyst for innovations in the system as a whole; that is, they would introduce new curricula, new subjects, and new teaching methods and spread these to non-state schools. Not all such private schools, however, were innovative, and some were even criticized for compromising quality for profit. The Ministry of Education is attempting to improve the monitoring of private school operations by making school salary and operation grants contingent upon a detailed year-end report. The private secondary technical schools drew particular criticism for following certain popular training trends, such as management, information technology, and business education, rather than assuming a truly innovative role (OECD, 1996).

The community: growing advocacy for children with special needs

The interviews uncovered numerous personal accounts from administrators, educators, and other parents whose children had failed to thrive under the rigid structure of the communist system because they did not fit the 'norm'. These were the individuals who established private schools for children with special needs, worked in advocacy groups (such as the *Blue Key School* for the rights of multiply-challenged youth), or founded parent organizations such as *Rytmus*[7] to lobby the government for the integration of mentally disabled students in state schools (Baxová, 1997; Černá, 1997; Hrubý, 1997; Jelínková, 1997). These parents and educators knew from personal experience that the old system was particularly harmful to some children and that changes were necessary. Their drive and unswerving determination were powerful forces in bringing these changes about (Mays *et al.*, 1997). As one interviewee explained, the uniqueness of the change process as it manifests in special education in the Czech Republic is that it is almost exclusively a spontaneous, grass-roots-initiated phenomenon, supported by charismatic individuals committed to making a difference in the lives of this neglected group (Kotásek, 1997).

Special-education advocates in the Czech Republic are beginning to see some positive developments in the field. For example, mandatory education for students with cognitive challenges was recently extended from eight years to thirteen; teachers have been given greater freedom to develop new, more flexible curricula that better meet the social needs of children with behavioural or emotional problems; increased parental involvement has been encouraged in the diagnosis of and programme planning for children and youth; more at-risk and troubled youth are being reintegrated in mainstream classrooms; and educators are beginning to take a more humanistic, ecological perspective that favours more adaptive programming and talent development for students (Polyzoi and Černá, 1999).

Numerous factors external either to the Czech Republic or to the school system pressed for change: the fall of Communism in Eastern and Central Europe, the influence of Western literature and scholars in the Czech Republic, efforts by national reform organizations, and the increasing voice of community members, particularly advocates for the rights of children with special needs. However, although islands of change have appeared, the Czech education system still lacks a conceptually coherent reform policy.

---

7 According to the association's founder, Pavla Baxová (personal communication, May 19, 2000), *Rytmus* means 'rhythm'; the name was selected to reflect the association's dynamic and evolving nature.

The degree to which change is supported by parents, students, and teachers

Cautious participants in the change process

In 1993, new education legislation establishing school-based management sought to encourage parental participation on the newly created school boards. However, many of these boards were characterized by apathy arising from parents' concerns that the boards' proposals for a more liberal education would negatively affect their children's success in passing entrance exams to the next level (Mays *et al.*, 1997). At a state care institution for moderately challenged adolescents which we visited in Doubraocany, the administration had made numerous attempts to involve parents in the decision-making process affecting services to their children, but had consistently met with resistance. Parents were quick to point out that their children's care was the responsibility of the state (and by implication of the institution), not of the parents (Fanta, 1997). At present, there are no powerful parent associations in the Czech Republic, although parental involvement in some (particularly non-state) schools is growing. Parents' traditional mistrust towards the school – inherited from the past regime – is slowly being replaced by a growing awareness that parents can exert a positive influence on school matters (Černá, 1997).

The extent of student involvement in the educational reform process is even less clear. The lack of empirical data about the role of Czech students in educational change makes it difficult to assess whether they embrace or reject the basic principles of the ministry's experimental programmes.[8] It is likewise unclear whether students support the innovations adopted by their particular schools. Nevertheless, it is assumed that students accept change more than teachers, because youth are less conditioned by old Soviet-era influences than are members of the older generation (OECD, 1996).

---

8 Since 1993–94, about a quarter of the Basic Schools have been experimenting with one of three new optional programmes. The 'General Curriculum' (Obecná Škola), designed for students in grades one to five and its counterpart, the 'Civic Curriculum' (Občanská Škola), designed for students in grades six to nine were introduced in 1993–94. The new 'Basic School' curriculum was introduced in March 1996, and the 'National School Curriculum' was introduced in March 1997. These new curricula represent a positive shift towards a more child-centred classroom, the relaxation of rigid teaching timetables, and alternative methods of teaching and evaluation (Jeřábek, 1997). The National School Curriculum was developed by the Association of Teachers of Basic Schools and is the most progressive (Nováčková, 1997). However, some believe that these programmes are still dependent on the traditional concept of the curriculum, i.e. facts rather than creative thinking and problem solving (Hausenblaus, 1997; Kotásek, 1997; Nováčková, 1997). The Ministry of Education, particularly as a response to curricular diversification, is currently considering the introduction of 'standards' as a means of assuring quality and comparability across school programmes. Until now, however, opinions have been diverse, even conflicting (OECD, 1996; Jeřábek, 1997).

Fullan notes it is ultimately the teachers – the front-line agents of change – who are critical to successful implementation of change. In the Czech Republic, individual teachers have often been the initiators of educational change. The successful introduction of new course content or teaching methods promoting a more liberal, child-centred philosophy has been largely due to these innovative-minded teachers (Kašová, 1997).

The majority of teachers in the Czech school system, however, remain cautious participants in the change process. While the attitude of teacher unions towards educational reform has not been entirely negative, these unions were opposed to massive liberalization of schools (OECD, 1996). In some instances, teachers may simply have been resisting 'bad' change; however, it is not unlikely that others preferred the centralized, prescriptive curriculum because it not only provided homogeneity and comparability across schools but also protected teachers from the risks inherent in making choices and expressing views. Education legislation introduced since 1989 has brought an end to mandatory curricula and textbooks in state schools and has provided teachers with more choices. However, it is difficult to assess the extent to which curricular autonomy at the school level has influenced the quality of teaching. Kalous (1997) estimates that only 10 per cent of schools have produced significant curricular innovations, and speculates that in most schools teaching methods have not significantly changed, whether because of time constraints, lack of external resources, or inadequate outside guidance. Much classroom learning has remained teacher-directed and fact-based; pupils continue to be assigned a passive role, and learning outcomes are expected to mirror what has been taught in the classroom. As one OECD observer commented during a visit to a number of schools in the Czech Republic in the fall of 1995: 'The school curricula may have changed, but the basic philosophy has remained the same' (OECD, 1996, p. 123).

Fullan indicates that 'individual teachers and single schools can bring about change without the support of central administrators, but district-wide [and by implication, nation-wide] change will not happen' (Fullan, 2001, p. 81). In some Czech schools, change has occurred as a result of lateral diffusion. However, innovation by teachers and active support by parents and students remain largely isolated and uncoordinated (Kašová, 1997). Moreover, since schools often compete for funds and students, little information sharing takes place among innovative programmes (Hausenblaus, 1997; Kalous, 1997; Nováčková, 1997). Unfortunately, pockets of change and isolated instances of innovation are not enough to profoundly transform Czech education.

Discussion

An exhaustive analysis of the process of transformation in the Czech Republic is beyond the purview of this study. Rather, the main objective of this chapter is to evaluate the utility of Fullan's conceptual framework for understanding Czechoslovakia's implementation of change after the Velvet Revolution. Clearly, the data support the value of his framework. Although legislative changes in the Czech Republic progressed fairly quickly, broader systemic change has proceeded more slowly, hindered by the absence of a clear vision. The heritage of the Communist regime, the waning influence of national reform groups, and the daunting task of reculturing an entire education system all have posed considerable challenges. Foreign advisors and Western models of education played an important role as external change agents in the initial change process; yet there is evidence that reforms are entering unevenly into the Czech educational system. Private schools have served to fill the gaps created by the demands of a new labour market. However, the absence of long-term planning in the implementation of new policy has often resulted in a piecemeal approach to educational reform. Nevertheless, educators are beginning to adopt a more humanistic, child-centred curriculum, one focused on the development of critical skills, problem-solving, and diversification of curricular options.

Despite the richness and multivariate nature of Fullan's schema, it does not specifically address the dynamics of the change process itself. It does not adequately provide answers to such questions as: Why is there a tendency towards retrenchment after initial change? Why is there a manifest attempt to return to pre-war models? Why is transformation comparatively less difficult for some Eastern and Central European countries (e.g. the Czech Republic) than for others (e.g. Russia)? The field of organizational theory may offer answers to some of these questions and at the same time provide insight into the dynamic character of the change process itself (Venda, 1991, 1999). Valery Venda[9] has developed a conceptual model which can be applied to post-Soviet countries in transition. Venda's theory of transformation and its correlative principles are described below.

Basic principles in Venda's model of transformation

PRINCIPLE 1: Systems in transition are typically characterized by the co-existence of old and new structures (Bîrzea, 1994). Venda describes this phenomenon in terms of learning curves (see Figure 4) – a general law of learning which can be applied to any level: an individual student learning in the classroom, a teacher struggling to implement a new programme, a school division attempting to address new curricular directives from the ministry, or a nation dealing with the collapse of totalitarianism and the development of an educational reform agenda. Each curve represents the efficiency of the system as it transforms from its current state to a new state. Once change is initiated, the efficiency under the old state falls until a common ground between the two states is reached, when it climbs

---

9 Before defecting to the United States from Russia in 1990, Valery Venda was Director of the National Program on the Improvement of Higher Education at the Moscow Institute of Higher Education and Research. After serving a term at Harvard, he was offered a chair in Human Factors in Ergonomics at the University of Manitoba, Canada.

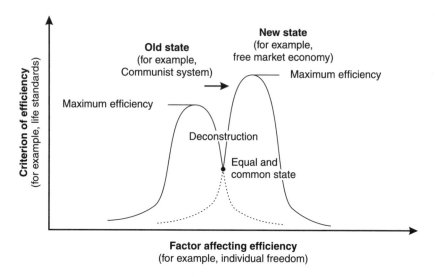

Figure 4 Illustration of the dynamics of system transformation.

again. The efficiency of the remaining part of the old state is obviously lower than that of its whole structure. However, on the basis of this common part, a whole new structure is synthesized and the efficiency of the new system rises to a higher level. The pulling-back of the education-reform movement in the Czech Republic may indicate a realization of the wisdom of a more cautious approach to change and an appreciation of the inherent complexity of the process.

In his 1994 study of post-Soviet countries, Bîrzea describes educational transformation as moving through the phases of *deconstruction, stabilization,* and *reconstruction.* In the weeks immediately following the Velvet Revolution, the old system was dismantled, new political and economic legislation was introduced, Marxism-Leninism was expunged from official school curricula, and the once rigidly controlled education system was dissolved. Bîrzea's schema appears to support and even extend Venda's first principle. In some post-Soviet countries (for example, Romania), there is, in fact, evidence of a *counter-reform* phase – a resurgence of communism which blocks or slows down the pace of educational reform.

PRINCIPLE 2: The emergent 'new' state may not have any elements in common with the 'old'; the wider apart the two states are initially (i.e. having no common or overlapping elements), the more difficult the transition process. It is evident that the Czech Republic's transition towards democracy was smoother than Russia's (see Polyzoi and Dneprov, Chapter 2). This is because the Czech Republic had maintained something of its pre-war infrastructure under Communist rule.[10] For Russia, following 70 years of Communism, the dynamic proc-

---

10 'Pre-war' refers to the period before World War II during the First Czechoslovak Republic, 1918–1939.

ess of deconstruction/reconstruction has been much more chaotic – punctuated by panic, demonstrations and even riots. In 1998, banks shut down, schools closed because teachers had not been paid for months, the rouble had become devalued, and the Russian people were thrown into an uncertain future (Nelan and Thompson, 1998). Venda postulates that when old and new states are too far apart, an intermediate state or bridge with features common to both must be constructed to span the gap in order to facilitate change (Figure 5). In the Czech Republic, the tendency to revive the old pre-Communist (and particularly pre-Occupation) models of education may represent an attempt to create such a bridge. Education is deeply rooted in the national history and traditions of the Czech Republic; in 1930, Czechoslovakia was a European leader in school reform. However, its reform attempts were interrupted by World War II, revived for three years following the war, and then destroyed again in 1948 by the Communist regime (Průcha and Walterová, 1992). Following the Velvet Revolution in 1989, innovative schools resurrecting models of the early twentieth century began to reappear (e.g. Waldorf, Rudolf Steiner, Montessori, and Society of Friends of Jan Hus schools) (Mays et al., 1997). However, these innovations were isolated and short-lived, as the impracticality of sustaining them was realized (Rýdl, 1997). On a broader level, even the country's reluctance to move quickly on reform initiatives may reflect the Ministry's effort to narrow the gap between the old, rigid and centralized education system and the new, decentralized and pluralistic one.

PRINCIPLE 3: If, as the old state begins to transform, its initial drop in efficiency is too steep (it is important not to slide down too fast), the system may enter a chaotic state and collapse. However, if the fall in efficiency is arrested

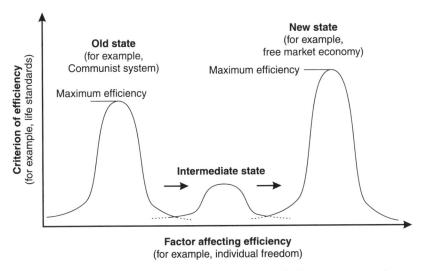

Figure 5 The creation of an intermediary state or bridge to facilitate transition when two states have few or no common elements.

early enough to prevent further erosion, the system can be stabilized. The nationwide dismantling of in-service teacher-training institutes left the Czech Republic with no means for training teachers; thus, it was a move which, ironically, threatened the very aim it was designed to promote. To redress this problem, the Ministry of Education allowed private enterprise to fill the void which its original directive created. If a new state is not well defined or if vision or long-term planning is lacking, transformation slows down considerably. Implementing ad hoc short-term solutions as problems arise, without considering the system as a whole, is not an efficient strategy for effecting change and may even be counter-productive. Such solutions often generate new problems, which in turn prompt further 'Band-Aid' solutions. Fullan (1999, p. 69) observes: 'because the development of capabilities takes time, it is essential that a mid- to long-term perspective be taken … [However] this has not been [a] politically attractive [strategy]. Policymaking is a world of adoption of the latest would-be solutions. It is a world of putting new policies "on the books" through legislation and other means. The timeline to the next election is always shorter than the timeline for capacity building.'

PRINCIPLE 4: The transformation process is not uni-dimensional but is affected by multiple factors occurring at the same time. Each factor, in effect, represents one dimension of the change process as it unfolds for each criterion of efficiency in the education system. These multiple factors, in concert, represent the interaction of external conditions and the internal adaptability of the educational structure. The factors identified in Fullan's framework, and used in this study as a schema for examining the Czech experience of the implementation of change, represent each dimension of the change process in Venda's framework. These factors include the specific nature of the reform, the character and strength of external factors which press for and facilitate change, and the degree to which change is supported at the local level by its direct participants or stakeholders. Each factor may be further broken down to the perceived need for and clarity of change, the influence of the past, the complexity of the change process, and so forth. For example, the stronger the need for change as perceived by teachers, the clearer the tenets of change, and the greater the administrative, community, and parental support for reform, the greater the ease with which a system can move towards the new state. Although criteria of system efficiency may conceivably include such items as teacher satisfaction, administrative efficiency, and students' academic performance, Fullan suggests that system efficiency may be interpreted as the capacity of a system (whether the unit of analysis is the school, district, or nation) to successfully manage innovation (Fullan, personal communication, March 23, 1999).[11] Building-in adaptability allows the organizational unit to be flexible, to continuously respond to a dynamic, living and evolving system – a

---

11 Fullan (1998, p. 69) defines local capacity building as 'directly and indirectly providing opportunities for advancing the knowledge, skills and work of local school and district personnel [in order to] create powerful learning communities', thus facilitating lasting change.

key ingredient for success. Fullan explains why capacity-building is so critical to successful reform: Knowledge must be grown not imposed; otherwise, it will fail. 'Successful reforms in one place are partly a function of good ideas and largely a function of the conditions under which the ideas flourished. Successful innovations ... fail to be replicated because the wrong thing is being replicated – the reform itself, instead of the conditions which spawned its success' (Fullan, 1999, p. 64).

In conclusion, Fullan's conceptual framework, while rich in detail, does not directly address the revolutionary nature of change. In addition, its representation of change is comparatively linear in character. Venda's transformational framework provides a dynamic overlay more consistent with an organic picture of the change process. Taken together, these two complementary models of change provide an enhanced understanding of the transition process, particularly when change is dramatic and sudden as in the case of former Communist countries in Eastern and Central Europe. The confluence of these models produces a dynamic picture of change that is much richer and more complex than either could yield by itself. As Fullan (1999, p. 79) aptly explains: 'The first ... step is to understand what makes social forces move forward in turbulent environments ... [This] involves understanding the complex interactive flow of change, establishing conditions that will turn this complexity into advantage, and then looking for, fostering, reinforcing and celebrating emerging outcomes that are valued, while discouraging those that are not ... Good outcomes are not as random as they may seem ... there are orientations that we can work on that make it likely that positive patterns will frequently emerge.' This study proposes a framework for thinking about change so that key forces can be identified and used to our advantage, particularly as they pertain to nations that undergo dramatic and sudden transformation.

References

Baxová, P. (1997) Interview by the primary author, Prague, May 11, 1997.

Beresford-Hill, B. (1998) Markets and education in Eastern Europe and the Baltic Republics. In P. Beresford-Hill (Ed.), *Education and Privatization in Eastern Europe and the Baltic Republics* (Series: *Oxford Studies in Comparative Education*) (pp. 9–19). Wallingford, Oxfordshire: Triangle Books.

Bîrzea, C. (1994) *Educational Policies of Countries in Transition.* Strasbourg: Council of Europe Press.

Černá, M. (1997) Interview by the primary author, Prague, May 21, 1997.

Dneprov, E. (1999) Interview by the primary author, Moscow, March 25, 1999.

Fanta, A. (1997) Interview by the primary author, Prague, June 18, 1997.

Fullan, M. (1993) *Change Forces: Probing the Depths of Educational Reform.* London: The Falmer Press.

Fullan, M. (1998, March) *What's worth fighting for out there?* Paper presented at the Conference on Student Assessment, Winnipeg, Manitoba, Canada.

Fullan, M. (1999) *Change Forces: The Sequel.* London: The Falmer Press.

Fullan, M. (2000) The return of large-scale reform. *The Journal of Educational Change,* 1(1), 1–23.

Fullan, M. (2001) *The New Meaning of Educational Change* (3rd edn). New York: Teachers College Press.

Gregor, V. (1997) Interview by the primary author, Prague, May 16, 1997.

Hausenblaus, O. (1997) Interview by the primary author, Prague, June 15, 1997.

Hrubý, J. (1997) Interview by the primary author, Prague, June 17, 1997.

Jelínková, V. (1997) Interview by the primary author, Prague, May 9, 1997.

Jeřábek, J. (1997) Interview by the primary author, Prague, March 29, 1997.

Kalous, J. (1997) Interview by the primary author, Prague, March 13, 1997.

Kašová, J. (1997) Interview by the primary author, Prague, June 26 1997.

Kotásek, J. (1997) Interview by the primary author, Prague, June 4, 1997.

Kovařovic, J. (1997) Interview by the primary author, Prague, June 20, 1997.

Mays, A., Polyzoi, E. and Gardner, S. (1997) The Czech experience of the initiation of educational change since 1989: is a North American model applicable? *Canadian and International Education,* 26(1), 32–53.

Ministry of Education, Youth and Sports of the Czech Republic (1994) *Quality and Accountability: The Programme of Development of the Education System in the Czech Republic.* Prague: Ministry of Education, Youth and Sports of the Czech Republic.

Nelan, B.W. and Thompson, M. (1998, September 7) Free fall: as Russia's economy melts, Yeltsin vows he will stay on. But to do what? *Time* [Canadian Edition], 152(10) 20–24.

Nováčková, J. (1997) Interview by the primary author, Prague, April 24, 1997.

OECD (1992) *Review on Higher Education in the Czech and Slovak Federal Republics.* Paris: Organization for Economic Co-operation and Development (OECD).

OECD (1996) *Review of National Policies for Education: Czech Republic.* Paris: Organization for Economic Co-operation and Development (OECD).

Pilátová, M. (1995) *The endless history of the kingdom of Bohemia.* Unpublished manuscript. Winnipeg: The University of Winnipeg.

Polyzoi, E. and Černá, M. (1999) Services for high-risk youth in the Czech Republic. *Reclaiming Children and Youth: Journal of Emotional and Behavioral Problems,* 7(4), 246–254.

Průcha, J. and Walterová, E. (1992) *Education in a Changing Society.* Prague, Czechoslovakia: Authors.

Rýdl, K. (1997) Interview by the primary author, Prague, June 16, 1997.

Venda, V. (1991) Transformation dynamics in complex systems. *Journal of the Washington Academy of Sciences,* 81(4), 163–184.

Venda, V. (1999) Interview by the primary author, Winnipeg, Manitoba, Canada, May 5, 1999.

4

EDUCATIONAL CHANGE AND SOCIAL TRANSITION IN HUNGARY

Gábor Halász, National Institute of Public Education, Budapest, Hungary

Scope and objectives

This chapter addresses recent reforms in Hungary's education system, particularly focusing on the regulation system, which has governed the national curriculum in the 1990s. These reforms are considered within the broader context of educational change to enhance our understanding of why and how reform occurs in education systems. As well, the case must necessarily be considered in terms of the larger social framework of transition from a non-democratic regime to democracy and a free-market economy. This chapter provides a critical analysis of the impact of the social transition on educational reform in Hungary, addressing those characteristics that distinguish the Hungarian case from other post-Soviet countries. More specifically, the analysis concentrates on those elements that are relevant to the theory of educational change presented in Fullan's conceptual framework (2001). It is argued that the change process, as experienced in Hungary, does not necessarily follow a linear pattern (as it does in North America); also that coherent outcomes may emerge from rather chaotic processes.

The case presented here has a number of unique features. First, it relates to a *major system change* with implications for all elements of education in Hungary. This change differs from that associated with one specific development project, or that confined to one organization or small group of schools. However, it is limited to one concrete component of the education system: curriculum regulation. Second, the change under analysis is *not yet fully complete* (if completion of change is a meaningful notion); that is, not all of its outcomes yet can be fully evaluated. Nevertheless, it has had a history of sufficient length to allow substantive analysis. Third, this reform was initiated during a period of *overall social-political transformation*. The broader context of change must be emphasized, particularly since it has had a major impact on the initiation and implementation of change, and certainly will affect its sustainability.

In Hungary, the process of transition from communism to democracy and

55

free-market economy has differed in many respects from the experience of other countries of the former Soviet Bloc. Free-market mechanisms and genuine civil initiatives first appeared many years before political transformation, which proceeded more smoothly in Hungary than in other Soviet-Bloc countries. Most of the institutional conditions for a market economy (e.g. company law, market-friendly tax system, bank reform, etc.) as well as basic democratic institutions (parliamentary framework, laws governing associations and free expression, etc.) were created *before* the fall of communism, and proved to be rather stable, surviving three democratic elections and changes of government during the 1990s.

Transition within Hungary's education sector also exhibited distinctive characteristics. Years in advance of real political change, Hungary initiated the decentralization of its educational administration, sometimes going much further than might have seemed possible within the framework of a communist state. The tension between the goals of restoration and modernization has been a prominent feature of educational transformation in Hungary. According to Radó (1999), an important aspect of the educational transition process in the former Soviet satellite countries – and indeed the motive for change – has been the desire to 'catch up' with Western Europe. Yet, 'Europeanization' – even when explicitly identified as a major goal (Kreitzberg, 1998) – has sometimes connoted more a desire to restore 'traditional European values' than a genuine wish to modernize the system. A particular feature of transition in Hungary has been a relatively strong commitment to modernization, as exemplified by the fact that when the conservatives came to power in the late 1990s, they retained most elements of the education modernization policies initiated by the liberals.

Despite the unique features of the Hungarian process of change, the notion of *transition* as defined by Bîrzea (1994) still applies to Hungary. According to Bîrzea, transition is necessarily accompanied by a certain degree of *anomie* or *instability*, which cannot be neutralized by the goals towards which the transition process strives (i.e. a working democracy and a free-market economy). More than a decade after the collapse of the communist regimes, one must still speak in terms of a transition period in new Central- and Eastern-European democracies, including Hungary.

Key concepts

One of the key concepts addressed in this chapter is *curricular regulation*. Educational systems are regulated through specific mechanisms (administrative, legal, financial, professional, etc.) and one of the goals of educational reform may be a change in these mechanisms. Within an education system, issues of regulation can arise in many areas (e.g. teaching and learning, student enrolments, resource allocation, etc.). In this chapter, the focus of analysis is the regulation of curriculum, i.e. the way that the content of teaching and the delivery of this content are determined and controlled. Changing the mechanisms of curriculum regulation may mean either *reallocating the responsibility* for curricular decisions to different stakeholders or system levels, or modifying the instruments that the different stakeholders (the state, for example) can use to determine the content and the delivery of teaching. This notion is closely related to *control* as defined, for example, by Weiss (1988), or to *integration* as used by Clark (1983),[1] but is connected more with policy than with systems theory. Regulation, in this case, is understood as a function of policy, which may be reformed in order to make a system more efficient for or accountable to democratic control.

A second key concept in the current analysis is *transition*. Following Bîrzea (1994) and Radó (1999), this chapter stresses four key features of transition: (1) it is a process of moving from one system (non-democratic) to an *entirely different* one (democratic), (2) it is accompanied by *crises and radical structural readjustments*, (3) it is accompanied by *uncertainty and destabilization*, and (4) it is fundamentally mitigated by the more or less well-defined *goals and directions* (market economy, modernization, etc.).

A third key concept addressed is that *change* is a positive phenomenon, to be understood as a response or adaptation to challenge. As emphasized earlier, this study also aims to contribute to the theory of educational change, as used by Fullan (2001). In the analysis of the Hungarian experience, Fullan's framework is applied, suggesting an enriched conception of the initiation-implementation-outcome/continuation chain.

The author, in attempting to understand the nature of reform, takes a middle position between those who maintain that changes are initiated and controlled by well-defined *social actors*, and those who believe that they are determined by *structural conditions*. Following Archer (1979), we believe that educational changes can only be adequately explained if both the '… complex kinds of *social* interactions whose result is the emergence of particular forms of education' and the 'complex types of social and educational *structures* which shape the context' are taken into account. This article, therefore, will address both.

The Hungarian experience

Hungary is a medium-sized Central European country of 10 million inhabitants covering an area of 93,000 square kilometres. After centuries of independence, followed by a long period of Ottoman occupation, Hungary became part of the Austrian Empire in the seventeenth century, and later a component of the Austro-Hungarian Monarchy; following World War I, it again became an independent state. After World War II, it came under Soviet control and remained part of the Soviet Bloc for 50 years. Since 1989, Hungary has been a parliamentary democracy. The first free elections (in 1990) were won by the national conservative

---

1 Clark uses the term 'integration' to explain how complex higher education systems operating under strongly divergent forces are brought together. According to Clark's analysis, the major integrating forces are the state, the market, and the academic oligarchy.

parties, then in 1994, a liberal-socialist coalition came to power. The third free elections took place in 1998 and were again won by the conservatives. The first half of the 1990s was characterized by a deep economic crisis, which led to high inflation and a sharp decrease in production, employment, and living standards. Recovery started in the second half of the decade and since 1997, there has been a relatively high level of economic growth accompanied by a macro-economic equilibrium.

Education, naturally, is only one of the sectors affected by the radical transformation process. Change has affected almost all areas of education: from the decision-making structures to curriculum content, and from the structural characteristics of the system to the status of the teaching profession. Curriculum policy is one of those areas in which changes were perhaps most spectacular and also most controversial. The 1993 Education Act suspended the enforcement of detailed centrally mandated curricular programmes, and introduced a two-level regulation system. The new regulations (outlined in separate documents) consisted of two key components: the central or national curriculum providing an overall educational framework, and the school-level curriculum directly regulating classroom processes.

The 1993 Education Act required that, within three years of publication of the national-level documents, every school was to prepare its own local documents. These were to consist of a school-specific 'pedagogical programme' as well as the 'local curriculum'. The former was conceived as a kind of general institutional-level strategy elaborated by the teaching staff, based on evaluation of the particular conditions of a given school and defining specific educational goals (e.g. the fight against school failure, preparation for higher studies, etc.). The second was to be a detailed, school-level plan, which includes timetables and subject matter specifications. This policy postulated that a nationally created assortment of programmes would permit schools to choose between creating their own local curricula, and simply applying or adapting existing programmes.

At the time these decisions were made, the form that the national-level documents were to take was still in the discussion stages. It was assumed that the government would provide a general framework, allowing sufficient room for schools to create their own local documents. The new national document, called the National Core Curriculum (NCC), was issued in 1995, two years after the new Education Act was introduced, and following a long period of public debate. One of the outcomes of this debate was the rejection of the original idea of two central curricular regulatory documents (one specifying general principles and the other containing the detailed contents and requirements of the school-based curriculum); the NCC document combined the two.

The drive to embody contemporary educational trends in the NCC was led by progressive educators in Hungary who were influenced by recent international developments in curricular theory. The NCC devoted much attention to the so-called *cross-curricular areas*: communication, health education, information and telecommunication technology, technical/practical skills, environmental protection, etc. Rather than defining traditional academic subjects, it defined ten *broader areas of knowledge* (e.g. 'Man and Society', 'Man and Nature'). It formulated *general* requirements guiding the development of each knowledge area in both the elementary (grades 1–6, ISCED 1) and lower-secondary (grade 7–10, ISCED 2) cycles. The requirements were defined as a function not of type or level of school but of student age. *Detailed* curricular outcomes were specified only for grades 4, 6, 8 and 10, rather than for every school year. This allowed individual schools to introduce adaptable timetables and allocate flexible blocks of time to specific knowledge areas. The NCC document did not stipulate the exact number of hours to be devoted to each area; only *lower* and *upper limits* were indicated. All these changes provided a high level of flexibility within the school system.

A 1996 amendment to the Education Act specified the content of the *pedagogical programme* as well as the *local or school-level curriculum*. According to this amendment, the school-level curriculum was required to define the following: (a) timetables (i.e. the list of subjects to be taught at various grade levels and the number of lessons to be devoted to each); (b) academic requirements or attainment targets for each subject; and (c) forms and procedures for evaluating students. The pedagogical programme and the local curriculum were first to be adopted by the teaching staff, and later – after external evaluation by nationally accredited experts – to be approved by the local municipality running the school. The design of school-level documents was not regulated by law, but rather left to the influence of non-legal documents, i.e. proposals and plans elaborated by various professional bodies.

By 1998, every school had prepared and received municipal approval for its local documents. The process was supported by the diverse contributions of various external actors (e.g. pedagogical support institutions, which provided professional advice). The character of these changes became the subject of intense professional and political debate. The key players in the new educational policy – politicians, researchers, professional pressure groups, etc. – were divided on whether the new form of curriculum regulation would ensure quality; they also were concerned about its impact on the uniformity of education across the nation. After a 1998 change of government, national surveys were conducted to assess the new legislation's impact; as a result, significant modifications were made. Some of these pushed the system into directions that diverged from the original document's intent. The majority of the modifications, however, helped stabilize the new environment that emerged from the changes, and were instrumental in the institutionalization of change. The most important change – prescribed by the 1999 Modification of the Education Act – was the addition to the NCC of a new regulatory document called *Frame Curricula* (FC). A number of new elements were also added to the rules governing pedagogical programmes – particularly in the areas of evaluation and ensuring of quality.

In 1999 and 2000, professional teams led by the Ministry of Education undertook elaboration of the FC. The new law required schools to revise their local curricula by the year 2001 to comply with the FC. The new regulatory document reintroduced specific subjects (e.g. physics, chemistry, history) into the ten broad knowledge areas, and reinstated annual timetables. It also readjusted academic requirements to bring them into alignment with the programme cycles of existing institutions (i.e. the 8-year basic schools and the 4-year gymnasia), dropping the earlier age-linked definition. The NCC remained in place as a national document, but most of its regulatory functions were transferred to the FC. The two-level system of regulation – obliging every school to prepare its own regulatory documents within the broader framework of a centralized curriculum – was preserved.

In tandem with the FC, a new ministerial decree was issued to regulate the preparation of school-level documents. This new regulation left room for a variety of deviations from the FC; for example, schools could, if they wished, continue teaching integrated subjects and interdisciplinary areas, instead of teaching specific subjects, as prescribed by the FC. It also provided a *system of accreditation*, which allowed schools to preserve their own local programmes, provided these were of high quality and nationally recognized – even if they departed substantially from FC guidelines.

An analysis of the process of change using Fullan's conceptual framework

The process of reforming the structure of curriculum regulation in Hungary cannot be described as linear in nature; the agents of change did not have clear objectives as they introduced and implemented reform. An external observer may well be astonished by the contradiction between the number of divergent initiatives involved in the change process, on the one hand, and the ultimate coherence of the outcome, on the other. Indeed the most intriguing question raised by an examination of the Hungarian case may be, '*How can a chaotic environment produce a rather coherent outcome?*' An attempt is made to answer this question by analyzing the change process, using Fullan's enriched linear change schema, and adapting it to the specific case of Hungary.

Initiation

One of the characteristics of the 'initiation' phase of change is the difficulty of assigning an exact moment to its commencement or of identifying its key agents. Certainly, cursory examination of events may suggest particular incidents or individuals as 'the' precipitating acts or agents of change, however, historical hindsight may reveal a different picture.

The history of educational reform in Hungary can be traced back to the mid-1970s. Following the Communist Party's 1972 political decision to introduce broad curricular reform, the education minister realized the potential benefit of consulting the Hungarian Academy of Science, Hungary's main scientific body, for advice. The minister felt that academia could lend impetus to the slow progress of educational reform. This was, in fact, what happened. Academy scientists prepared a report, the *White Book*, containing a number of reform proposals, however, these were seen as too progressive, and were ultimately rejected. Nevertheless, the principles embodied in the report had a lasting influence on Hungary's educational system.

Although it may be difficult to give unequivocal credit for the initiation of reform initiative to specific persons or groups, a number of key individuals can be identified. Of these, a four-member team of recognized curriculum experts with significant international experience made an outstanding contribution. The members of this team were: Zoltán Báthory, József Nagy, Endre Ballér and Péter Szebenyi – all university professors. In the early 1970s, as young researchers, three of them participated in a seminar organized by the International Association for the Evaluation of Educational Achievements (IEA), and were strongly influenced by what they learned about curriculum theory. Zoltán Báthory, as Deputy State Secretary, was responsible for school education between 1994 and 1998, during which time the NCC was issued and school-level reform was implemented. It was this group which, in the late 1980s, suggested the creation of a new national curriculum (Nagy and Szebenyi, 1990; Báthory, 1993).

A number of individuals played important roles in the reform of *vocational* training. Emergent crises in the dual-training system[2] and the strong need (as a consequence of economic restructuring) for structural readjustment in the education domain made the call for reform particularly acute in this sector. The World Bank financed a reform programme, which supported the lengthening of the general phase of technical and vocational secondary education from eight to ten years; the curricular goals set by this programme (e.g. integration, longer general education, etc.) were very similar to those of the NCC. Consequently, those in the vocational training sphere, who admired the success of the World Bank programme, also supported the NCC reform initiatives.

It is important to note one additional group influential in the reform of Hungarian education: *teacher groups* or professional associations. Recognizing that the new two-tier regulation model would serve to extend their professional autonomy, these groups became natural supporters of the reform. Endorsement was particularly strong among those committed to progressive or (as they often referred to it), *alternative* pedagogy. Some teacher groups became supporters of radical reform; their revolutionary views often caused schisms within the larger body of educational supporters.

However, teachers were not unanimous in their approval of reform. Such resistance to reform may be understood in part as stemming from fear that enhanced public involvement in school-level curricular change would increase external control over the individual teacher. A significant proportion of teach-

---

2   The dual-training system combined school-based education and practical workplace training; until 1989, it enrolled approximately 50 per cent of an age cohort.

ers expressed nostalgia for the former centralized model. This was understandable: any reform, which enhances public involvement in school-level curricular change, implies increased external control over the individual teacher. Furthermore, although NCC was conceived as an instrument for achieving coherence out of diversity, the fact that it was to be used in a decentralized context made many teachers think it was the *cause* of diversity.

It is unclear whether *resources* played any role in the reform process. If so, it could be said that the introduction of the decentralized regulation model was more an answer to a shortage of resources than an attempt to utilize newly available ones. The economic crisis of the early 1990s led to a scarcity of resources, which made it impossible to maintain the usual operation of schools. Since the state could no longer provide them with necessary resources, it gave schools the freedom to find alternative sources – even if this meant tolerating modifications to pedagogical activities.

It is particularly important to note, however, that the state did not just (to use an apt Hungarian adage) 'throw the reins between the horses' during the reform process. Scarcity of resources can often be managed by strengthening control. The Hungarian government made a more-or-less explicit strategic decision to maintain the *dynamism and adaptive capacity* of the system even at the cost of losing some degree of control over local processes. In spite of serious operational problems caused by lack of funds, a number of decisions were made to re-deploy resources from daily school operations to curriculum development.

Administrators responsible for ensuring the appropriate operation of the system also played an important role. The 1985 Education Act made it possible for schools, if authorized, to apply the so-called 'particular curricular solutions' (i.e. deviations from the official curriculum). Thanks to liberal authorization policies, school-level curriculum modifications proliferated by the early 1990s. The existing regulation framework became dysfunctional as the high number of curricular exceptions eventuated in an uncontrollable curricular field. By the early 1990s, there was a strong need for a new regulatory framework capable of simultaneously assuring coherence and accommodating diversity.

After the 1990 Law of Self-Government granted ownership of former state schools to local communities, the contradiction intensified between the new decentralized system of public administration and the unchanged mechanisms of curriculum regulation. Schools were now owned and controlled by autonomous local municipalities; however, the centralized system of curriculum control continued, without appropriate curriculum control instruments. Since inspection – the main venue for regulation – was abolished as early as 1986, the central bureaucracy could no longer take full responsibility for school curricular processes. A more flexible regulation framework was seen as a logical solution.

As in all education systems, the need to periodically update the content of teaching in order to keep pace with developments in culture and the sciences was another factor in the drive for reform. Modernization of teaching content had not been undertaken since the late 1970s, when the latest overall reform of curriculum had taken place. Curriculum specialists, concerned about obsolete teaching content and heavy course loads, urged reform. They suggested the creation of a new national curriculum by the end of the 1980s, proposing as a first step the modernization of teaching and learning, rather than reshaping of regulation mechanisms. This factor is particularly significant because it contributed to an important characteristic of change, namely, *floating goals*, that allowed educators to concentrate on renewing teaching content instead of changing the curriculum regulation system.

International influences also played an important role in the change process. The earlier-named experts who were influential in Hungary's educational reform movement had substantial knowledge of the international scene; as well, some external agencies (e.g. the World Bank, the Council of Europe, and the OECD) and certain countries (e.g. the United Kingdom), had considerable impact on the reform process. Nevertheless, the model of curriculum reform that emerged in Hungary was purely an internal product.

The existence of *earlier innovations* also was important in paving the way for the initiation of educational change in Hungary. In a rigid, centralized system, curricular innovations often are introduced as 'experiments'. This has been the case in Hungary since the first small-classroom model was authorized in the 1970s. The establishment of an experimental school in the southern village of *Szentlőrinc* was one of the most influential initiatives of the time, first demonstrating that deviation from the mainstream need not lead to chaos – although it may precipitate conflict and tension.

As mentioned earlier, by the beginning of the 1990s, local curricular changes proliferated within the education system. This proliferation was deliberately encouraged by certain national initiatives. In 1988, the establishment of a national development fund (KÖFA) allowed schools to submit proposals for innovative programmes and obtain financial support for their implementation. Through such national funding, schools could acquire resources not controlled by the local municipality. At the same time, the central administration's support legitimated initiatives for change by schools within the rather change-resistant local environment. Schools also learned to deal with the organizational tensions that necessarily arise when change is introduced. Thanks to KÖFA, the number of 'innovation islands' was already very high by the late 1980s.

Finally, it is important to recognize the *macropolitical factors* in the initiation of educational change in Hungary. Although the two-level curriculum regulation model was legislated in 1993 under a conservative government, the detailed instrument (NCC) was issued and implemented between 1995 and 1998 when the Ministry of Education was under liberal control. The strong commitment of liberals to curricular freedom and modernization has had a major impact on both the initiation and the implementation phases of educational reform.

Implementation

Implementation is a strong determinant of the fate of reform ideas. Historical analyses often give much more attention to the birth of such ideas than to the crucial matter of their implementation. However, it is this phase of educational reform which deserves the closest scrutiny.

The macroeconomic, societal, and structural environment of change. A number of factors related to the broader macroeconomic and societal contexts had a destabilizing effect on Hungary's education system and strongly influenced the change process. These factors were not necessarily related to the phenomenon of transition (defined earlier). The initiation of curriculum regulation reform in Hungary took place within the context of regional *economic crisis* endemic to the whole former Soviet Bloc. The economy had been stagnant for more than a decade, and reform started at the nadir of an economic crisis compounded by a sharp decline in economic activity and output over several years. In the first half of the 1990s, the workforce shrank from more than 5.2 million to 3.8 million people. In 1995, the GNP was only 84 per cent of what it had been in 1987. Public institutions, including schools, were subjected to particularly severe budget cuts; as a result, the real value of teacher salaries fell significantly between 1994 and 1996 (National Institute of Public Education, 1998).

Another factor leading to destabilization in the institutional environment was the dramatic *demographic decline* in Hungary during this period. Between 1975 and 1990, the size of the six-year-old age cohorts decreased by more than 40 per cent. This led not only to a real threat of school closures and/or staff reductions, but also to an intensified competition among schools for pupils and resources.

The implementation of the new curriculum regulation model was also strongly contingent upon a number of structural constraints within the existing education system. Independent of the regulation pattern introduced by the government, many of these constraints had a direct impact on the shape that the new curriculum could take. The most important of the structural changes was the appearance of new types of schools, which offered a different length (number of years) of study than pre-existent schools. This necessitated the modification of the *vertical structure* of the educational system. Before 1990, all students completed eight years of basic education. Under the new structure, an increasing number of secondary schools started enrolling pupils after grades four and six. This development inevitably raised fundamental questions of *comprehensiveness* (i.e. How long should general studies for all last?). This question was to be partially addressed by the new curriculum regulations. Proponents of two opposing views offered solutions: the first group advocated maintaining or extending the original length of comprehensive schooling; the second, which approved of structural differentiation, supported alternative (e.g. advanced and normal level) curricula for lower grades.

A *horizontal* structural change with curricular implications was related to the rapid expansion of enrolment in general secondary programmes and the fall of enrolment in ninth- and tenth-grade vocational training. Due to attendant changes in the social composition and academic capacities of the respective student populations, certain teaching contents and requirements became inapplicable.

The national government retained only partial control over structural change. It loosened national regulation of the school structure (authorizing, for example, new vertical models), and suspended formal central planning of enrolment in different (i.e. general vs. vocational) profiles. Decisions on vertical structural arrangements (i.e. number of grades) and individual school profiles were delegated to the local level.

These changes modified the context in which curriculum regulation was to operate. As well, they loaded the educational discourse with themes related to class structure and social reproduction (the reason being that some of the new school forms – secondary academic schools enrolling 10- and 12-year-olds – assumed the explicit role of moulding the social elite). Curriculum's function as a structural regulator came to the fore. Some advocates of a more prescriptive regulation pattern believed it would reinforce the system's structural unity; at the other extreme were those who favoured the extension of general basic education and sought a looser regulation as a means to that end.

One of the most serious systemic structural conflicts within education systems is between the general and the vocational-technical sub-sectors. The Hungarian case study presents a rare example of reform endeavours in which the general and the vocational education sectors reinforced one another. During the 1990s, the vocational sector had favoured lengthening the general phase of education and deferring specialization to the upper grades; this harmonized with the goals of the NCC reform.

Characteristics of implementation. The success of reform implementation depends on a number of elements. In his conceptual framework, Fullan (2001) identifies four major factors: (1) need, (2) clarity, (3) complexity, and (4) quality/practicality of the proposed change.

The 'need' factor is not easy to evaluate. Although a new content-regulation system was clearly needed by the mid-1990s, whether the form adopted by the NCC best served that need was less clear. Furthermore, needs are perceived subjectively. An external observer may insist that both teachers and schools have a need for curriculum regulation reform; teachers, however, may not share this view.

'Clarity' is much easier to evaluate. Although the regulation system proposed in the NCC was quite clear and coherent, it departed strikingly from past practice. Study and reflection were required in order to grasp the new system's coherence. This suggests that clarity is a moving notion: at the end of the implementation process, the direction and the content of change were much clearer than at the beginning. It must be noted that the government made deliberate efforts to clarify both the nature of the changes and the implementation process itself; to this end, it introduced a separate strategy for implementation (Põcze, 1995).

A new regulation system is a highly *complex* change. Albeit, sometimes it is not the reform being introduced that is complex, but rather the situation that it was intended to address. In the case presented here, both situation (a decentralized, diversified system with an inherited centralized regulation mechanism), and solution (a new two-level regulation system) were complex.

Evaluating the 'quality and the practicality' of change is also a complicated task, partly, again, because of the subjective nature of how the context and the solution are perceived. For example, teachers desirous and capable of working independently may welcome the NCC regulation model; those needing greater direction and supervision in their professional activities may find it less appropriate.

The success of implementing any reform is also determined by the richness, coherence, and synergy of the *actions* and *instruments* used by the reformers during the implementation phase. In this case, a large number of instruments were mobilized in the reform initiative, and efforts were made to ensure coherence among them.

A national *supply of curricular programmes* was created and made available to schools, which could adapt and use them as local curricula. Significant resources were placed at the disposal of development agencies that could produce such programmes for the Ministry of Education. In order to ensure coherence, a national *standard format* was elaborated and an electronic *communication network* created to facilitate the transfer of information to schools.

A new *in-service training system* was created and provided with ample resources. All potential training-providers were mobilized from teacher-training colleges and pedagogical support institutions to pilot schools and private training consulting companies. In general, learning, communication, and capacity building were encouraged at all levels.

The central *development fund* was renewed, and the resources placed at its disposal significantly increased. Calls for tenders were published for projects directly related to the reforms. Synergies were sought between the Programme for the Development of Education (a major educational development programme funded by the Soros Foundation) and the activities of the government's innovation fund. The Soros Foundation multiplied the resources available for educational development, and all proposed expenditures were submitted to a strategy concordant with the reforms.

The implementation process was, however, characterized by a number of *contradictions* and *paradoxes*. One of the most glaring is the fact that serious reflection about the implementation strategy of the new content-regulation system began only *after* implementation was under way. Post-implementation discussions revealed a number of difficulties which, had they been explored during the planning phase, might have influenced decisions made by the system's designers. As it was, the extent of the challenges faced by teachers in every school and the tremendous need for external support became clear only during the process of implementation itself.

Sometimes, decisions about resources were made before there was any clear understanding of how these would be deployed. For example, a 1996 amendment to the Education Act allocated extensive resources for in-service teacher training and even made such training compulsory; however, no concept yet existed of the system in which these resources were to be used or how these teachers could be trained.

The whole process of change was accompanied by various kinds of *uncertainties*. Because of the novelty of many elements, teachers, principals, and other educators raised a multitude of questions that the administration was incapable of answering. During the implementation period, a myriad of technical problems also arose, ranging from deadline problems and defects in the electronic communication network, to a lack of quality control.

Macropolitical influences also figured prominently in the implementation process. Frequent declarations by the opposition party that, if elected, they would significantly modify the new system caused many local administrators to feel uncertain about the outcome of the reform process and prompted them to adopt a 'wait-and-see' attitude.

Outcomes and institutionalization

Sustainability is a key problem in any change initiative. As Fullan (2001) points out: when the will to change diminishes or when funds are depleted, education reforms and change projects are often abandoned; pre-change conditions may even be restored. This is a particularly relevant matter in countries undergoing transition; once the transitional phase is over, some reforms may be viewed as the ephemeral phenomena of a period of instability or uncertainty.

Education reform in Hungary produced a number of important outcomes. Some, such as the mobilization of creative energies in schools and within the teaching profession, are clearly positive. Approximately one sixth of Hungarian schools produced new local curricula on their own, and only a few schools adopted centrally offered programmes without any significant local adaptation. According to a national survey of school principals (Szocio-reflex Kft, 1999), human relations within the teaching profession improved in almost one third of schools, and the professional quality of staff (as perceived by the survey respondents) improved in almost 70 per cent of the schools. The attitude of many teachers has changed towards the development of independent work. Recent analyses (e.g. Setényi, 2000) have demonstrated that the Hungarian system's openness to innovation and change has increased dramatically. Innovation has now become an institutionalized process, supported by an environment which produces regular incentives, and a teaching profession which responds to them positively. A recent study (OECD/CERI, 2000) summarizes the following outcomes of reform:

- increase in school's openness to community involvement;
- increased acceptance of cross-disciplinary approaches within the schools;
- expanded efforts to adapt school-level programmes to students' special needs;
- dramatic increase in the need for in-service training among teachers and principals;

- radical change in the traditional relationship between staff and principal;
- enhanced sense of professionalism among principals and teachers.

Reform, however, does not come without its share of negative outcomes (Balázs et al., 1998; Altrichter and Halász, 1999). The quality of school programmes is no longer guaranteed; according to some reports (e.g. Vágó, 2000), a relatively high number of schools produce low quality local programmes. Interestingly, the change process has also led to a modification of the definition of 'quality': growing emphasis is now placed on consumer satisfaction and less on national standards. Differences among schools – which had already been in evidence – have further increased. As a result, equality – ironically – has become the least achieved of the education policy goals.

Of paramount concern in matters of reform is to what extent changes will be sustained and/or institutionalized. Fullan (2001) identifies four essential factors in the sustainability of educational reforms beyond the implementation phase: (1) active participation of the various stakeholders, (2) community pressure and support, (3) clear changes in teacher behaviour, and (4) ownership of change. Within this conceptual framework, the Hungarian reform of curriculum regulation can be characterized as follows.

Through a number of major national and smaller local conferences, teacher participation in the lengthy pre-reform discussions had been extensive. Input from the professional public was also sought several times through a number of national surveys. Participation in the reform process itself was also high. According to a survey of school principals conducted following the preparation of the school-level pedagogical programmes (Szocio-reflex Kft, 1999), almost 50 per cent of the teaching staff had participated in the re-examination of their current programme, 31 per cent in the formulation of the pedagogical programme document, and 65 per cent in the preparation of timetables for each school subject.

External support was relatively strong, as was the push for change by various professional and social groups. Influential professional groups (e.g. curriculum-development advisers and innovative teachers) emerged in support of reform and exercised pressure on the administration to continue the process although pressure to slow down the pace of change was also strong. According to survey results (Vágó, 2000), at the peak of the implementation process in 1998, 60 per cent of teachers were in favour of reform. Over a period of time, massive attitudinal change has taken place among teachers. Through active collective work on school-level diagnosis, self-evaluation, and strategy development, teachers learned to integrate new ways of collegial interaction (e.g. working in teams on development projects) that has led to irreversible modifications in their professional behaviour. Finally, a sense of ownership has been relatively strong in those schools that have created their own curricula (17 per cent) or made serious adaptations to the centrally offered model programme (52 per cent). All these factors furnish evidence that change has become irrevocable and its continuation probable.

It should be noted, however, that the sustainability of reform is also strongly dependent on a number of *macropolitical changes*. As mentioned earlier, not all key players in the education-policy arena shared the view that a flexible, decentralized system of regulation would ensure a consistent or acceptable standard of quality. Although the conservatives, upon returning to power in 1998, did cut back the reforms, pre-change conditions were not restored. A number of measures were introduced which altered the original regulation model but did not transform its essential mechanism, i.e. the two-tier system and the devolution of goal-setting and programme-planning responsibilities to the schools.

Since their introduction, some elements of reform have even been further reinforced. In the debate on the balance between internal and external mechanisms for quality control, the internal model has clearly prevailed. In 1999, *Comenius 2000* (a major central programme with significant resources) was launched with the aim of introducing user-oriented, institutional-level *quality assurance mechanisms* (Ministry of Education, 2000), entirely in keeping with the spirit of the NCC model. More than one third of schools expressed willingness to participate in this programme.

Several additional factors make a return to pre-reform conditions highly unlikely. First, at the local level, the changes that have accumulated over time are already so substantial that re-introduction at this point of an inflexible regulation mechanism, incompatible with alternative solutions, would cause insurmountable administrative problems. Second, institutionalization of the outcomes of NCC implementation is already too advanced. Any radical return to pre-reform conditions would cause extreme destabilization. Third, results have shown that – in spite of all the problems – the new system is working and corrections are possible within the emerging new framework. Fourth, most of the support mechanisms (innovation funds, in-service training system, electronic communication networks, etc.) that were created to support change have been preserved and continue to impact on educational institutions. Finally, the international scene (i.e. developed countries in which reforms support decentralization and enhanced school-level autonomy) provides reinforcing feedback to Hungary. This is particularly true of the European Union education programmes, which became accessible to Hungary in the mid 1980s.

Taking all these factors into consideration, it can be stated with a high degree of certainty that the reform of curriculum regulation in Hungary is not an ephemeral feature of the nation's educational transition period. Although reform of a radical nature and so vast in scope might not have been possible during a period of social and political stasis, its sources cannot be traced exclusively to the particular conditions of social and political upheaval.

Discussion

Educational change in a society in transition necessarily presents characteristics that differ from those observed under more stable conditions. The analysis of educational reform in Hungary reveals a number of specific features, which can be summarized as follows.

1 *Educational changes are strongly related to processes external to the education sector.* This, of course, is more or less true for all contexts, including more stable societies. Reforms – such as decentralization in France or Sweden, school improvement or restructuring in the United States, or stronger national level involvement in the definition of curricula in the United Kingdom – cannot be explained exclusively in terms of factors internal to the education system. However, the inter-linkage between internal and external change factors is stronger in societies undergoing transition. In addition to the macropolitical changes, the following external factors have had significant impact on education reform in Hungary: economic restructuring and the subsequent crisis in the vocational-training sector; public-administration and public-financing reform; and demographic changes and consequent changes in enrolment structure.

2 *The change process is not linear.* As a result of the uncertainties characteristic of periods of transition, goals are often modified and the instruments available for achieving these goals also change. In the earlier stages of any reform, goals may not be clearly defined, implementation details may be obscure, and contradictions in views and approaches may not be explicit. In fact, alternative scenarios – which can lead to different outcomes – sometimes become clear only after change has taken place. In such circumstances, it is essential that change agents maintain flexibility, be perceptive to messages coming from the environment, and be prepared to compromise; i.e. to modify strategy according to changes in the environment. They must have a coherent value system in order to react to spontaneous developments in a coherent way. As has been demonstrated elsewhere (Halász, 1993), pre-reform conceptualization was very weak in Hungary; in this case, there were several serious shifts that occurred in the interpretation of goals and even in the direction of reform. However, a number of basic assumptions (e.g. school-level responsibility for curriculum) have never been questioned.

3 *The capacity to manage uncertainty is a critical factor.* Given the high level of uncertainty in contexts of societal transition, an important criterion for successful reform is the capacity of all leading agents of reform (including all participating institutions) to preserve, on the one hand, their internal coherence and commitment, and, on the other, to make necessary concessions and compromises. A balance must be maintained between the need for stable rules and the need to be open and versatile. This task requires individuals with strong professional and ethical commitment combined with pragmatic flexibility. In the Hungarian reform movement, the capacity of key individuals to manage the abundant uncertainties was quite strong. In fact, these individuals were compelled to confront a number of uncertainties well before real transition began, because of such factors as high demographic

fluctuations and deteriorating financial conditions. A typical experience of Hungarian school principals is illustrative: when the detailed, centrally defined rules of school operation were abolished in the 1980s, many principals had no choice but to prepare their own rules of organization and operation, without any central support.

4   *Greater willingness to take risk is endemic to societies in transition.* In transitional environments, it is easier to make high-risk decisions – and, therefore, to set more ambitious goals than might be set under normal circumstances. Experience shows that many successful solutions were considered audacious at the time they were proposed. As risk-taking increasingly becomes a norm in all spheres of social life, the likelihood diminishes of such behaviour being regarded as irresponsible. Risk-taking is needed because of the reluctance of the democratic culture to treat divergent views and the relative politicization of administration. Administrators identifying themselves with the reform line risk being 'sacked', if its opponents should take office. As analysts of educational management problems often point out, an important prerequisite for Hungarian school-leadership position is the risk-taking capacity.

5   *Communication and ongoing learning become particularly important.* In a rapidly evolving environment in which unforeseen factors may continually arise, enhanced communication becomes a key condition for successful change. All the participants are in a permanent learning situation, i.e. a situation characterized by an initial acceptance of ignorance accompanied by a continuous openness to new information. Among the most important features of the Hungarian change process are the increased need for communication and learning, and the creation of new venues (e.g. public debates, professional conferences, new electronic communication networks, expanded in-service training facilities, etc.) to satisfy this need.

6   *Efficiency in use of resources increases with experience.* Since the level of planning and preparation may be low, resources are often wasted. In Hungary, the continuous modification of goals and scenarios disrupted even long-term planning; for example, investment in the creation of programmes, textbooks, and school-level curricula in compliance with the NCC was partly lost with the advent of the FC. Teams of curriculum specialists working on the national documents were created and dissolved several times; in-service training programmes had to be modified with each appearance of new national documents. This pattern also led to fatigue and burnout among educators. However, the experience gained during all these travails was not lost. Ideas which emerged during the preparation of the NCC were transmitted to the FC committee; experience gained during the pre-1998 local negotiations on pedagogical programmes and local curricula will be valuable in future revisions of school-level documents.

7   *A pragmatic approach focusing on the instruments of implementation prevails over abstract, theoretical conceptions of change.* One of the distinctive features of the Hungarian reform process has been a relatively strong focus on the

technical issues of implementation. Abstract, theoretical discussions of regulation models did not characterize this phase. Indeed, rather the opposite:
sometimes solutions were presented as exemplifying a particular model only
subsequent to their practical application. Critics of Hungary's educational
reform process often complained that the publication of explicit conceptions
only occurred following the implementation of measures putatively based
upon them.

In summation, it is possible to formulate two major conclusions. First, broader
social transitions taking place within a nation may have both positive and
negative effects on educational change. On the one hand, transition naturally
facilitates changes in the education system; on the other, it may increase the
fragility of such changes. Therefore, particular attention must be given to those
factors that make the implementation of change more efficient and that lead to
its higher-level institutionalization. Second, the adequate description and explanation of educational change in environments of transition requires conceptual
frameworks, which are non-linear, unlike those applicable in more stable environments. Within this adapted framework, (a) change must be understood not
only as a goal but also as the outcome of an open process; and (b) the focus of
analysis (as defined by its initiators) must be shifted away from the original goals
of change and towards the environment, which not only determines whether or
not those goals will be achieved but also serves continuously to modify them.

References

Altrichter, H. and Halász, G. (1999) *Comparative analysis of decentralization policies and their results in Middle European Countries. Final Report.* Unpublished manuscript. Budapest – Linz.

Archer, M. (1979) *The Social Origins of Education Systems.* London: Sage Publications.

Balázs, E., Halász, G., Imre, A., Moldován, J. and Nagy, M. (1998) *Inter-governmental roles in the delivery of educational services – Hungary.* Unpublished manuscript. Budapest: National Institute of Public Education.

Báthory, Z. (1993) A national core curriculum and the democratization of public education in Hungary. *Curriculum Studies*, 1, 91–104.

Bîrzea, C. (1994) *Education Policies of the Countries in Transition.* Strasbourg: Council of Europe Press.

Clark, B. R. (1983) *The Higher Education System: Academic Organization in Cross-National Perspective.* Berkeley: The University of California Press.

Fullan, M. G. (2001) *The New Meaning of Change* (3rd edn). New York: Teachers College Press.

Halász, G. (1993) The policy of school autonomy and the reform of educational administration: Hungarian changes in an East European perspective. *International Review of Education*, 39(6).

Kreitzberg, P. (1998) Educational transition in Estonia, 1987–1996. In P. Beresford-Hill (Ed.), *Education and Privatization in Eastern Europe and the Baltic Republics* (Series: *Oxford Studies in Comparative Education*) (pp. 47–59). Wallingford, Oxfordshire: Triangle Books.

Ministry of Culture and Education Hungary (1996) *National Core Curriculum*. Budapest: Ministry of Culture and Education Hungary.

Ministry of Education (2000) *Comenius 2000: Quality Improvement Programme in School Education*. Budapest: Ministry of Education.

Nagy, J. and Szebenyi, P. (1990) *Curriculum Policy in Hungary*. Budapest: Hungarian Institute of for Educational Research.

National Institute of Public Education (1998) *Education in Hungary, 1997*. Budapest: National Institute of Public Education.

OECD/CERI (2000) *New school management approaches*. Hungary: OECD. Unpublished manuscript.

Põcze, G. (1995) A NAT és a gyakorlat. A Nemzeti Alaptanterv implementációja (The NCC and the practice. The implementation of the National Core Curriculum). *Új Pedagógiai Szemle*, **4**, 12–36.

Radó, P. (1999) *Transition in Education. The Key Education Policy Areas in the Central-European and Baltic Countries*. Budapest: Institute for Education Policy, Open Society Institute.

Setényi, J. (2000) *Study on What Works Innovation in Education: New School Management Approaches*. Budapest: Hungarian Background Report to OECD.

Szocio-reflex Kft (1999) *A nemzeti alaptanterv bevezetése, az iskolák helyi tanterve 1998 őszén (The implementation of the national core curriculum and the local curriculum of schools in the autumn of 1998)*. Unpublished manuscript. Budapest.

Vágó, I. (2000) Az oktatás tartalma (The content of education). In *Jelentés a magyar közoktatásról – 2000 (Report on school education – 2000)*. Budapest: National Institute of Public Education.

Weiss, J. (1988) Control in school organizations: Theoretical perspectives. In W. Clune and J. Witte (Eds), *Choice and Control in American Education* (pp. 91–134). Philadelphia: The Falmer Press.

5

REFORMING THE ROMANIAN SYSTEM OF EDUCATION

The agenda ahead

*Cesar Bîrzea, Director of the Institute of Education Sciences in Bucharest;
Professor, University of Bucharest
Ciprian Fartuşnic, Institute of Education Sciences (Educational System
Evaluation Department) and Romanian National Observatory*

Purpose

The pressure for change, which exists in an open society, is an important force in the transformation of an education system (Fullan, 2001). The experience of the former Communist countries of Central and Eastern Europe, in which the beginnings of education reform coincided with the emergence of democratic elements, would seem to support this thesis; thus, Hungary and Poland (in the 1970s and 1980s respectively) took their first steps towards the decentralization of their education systems. The reverse is also true; any closed society – once it has 'aligned' its educational system to its own ideological coordinates – accepts extremely few changes. In Romania, not until the dramatic and painful collapse of the Communist regime in December 1989, did the first major changes in its education system take place.

Once the democratic powers were instated, the Romanian public expected comprehensive educational reform, and this was not long in coming. The Ministry of National Education (the institution in charge of the general management of education and the final authority on school governance) was the principal promoter of reform. The Ministry of Finance and the Ministry of Labour also played significant roles in the design of educational policies. Various laws, ordinances, governmental decisions, application directives, analyses, and strategies were prepared with a view to transform an education system turned rigid and excessively centralized during the Communist years. At the political level, administrators openly admitted that education was essential for the nation's economic development and that schools represented an invaluable source of cognitive and technological innovation. Doctrinal differences did not prevent political parties from agreeing on the importance of education and making it a priority of their platforms in the first free elections (May 1990). Education remained a priority for the period to come, and the subject of public scrutiny and debate. The public welcomed foreign ideas and the education system benefited greatly from Romania's reconnection to the international scene (Carothers, 1999). Changes were aimed at establishing a society based on a free market economy, the rule of law, and individual freedom (OECD, 2000). According to policy analysts, these changes affected the entire education system, its programmes, actors, underlying philosophy and governance.

More than a decade after the initiation of reform, understanding the complex process of change in Romania's education system remains critical to moving the agenda forward. We need to assess the transformation of Romanian education: how profound and durable reform measures have been and how political, bureaucratic, and financial barriers threaten to diminish their success.

In this chapter, we attempt to gauge the success of the Romanian education system's attempts to consolidate the reform measures initiated in 1990. To do so, we shall explore the most important stages of the global reform of Romanian education and the strong underlying paradigm of change that has guided this process. We shall be looking at these from the perspectives both of Fullan's conceptual framework, and of our own understanding of the transition process in former communist countries (Bîrzea, 1994). Our approach combines concepts specific to the theory of educational change with close analysis of the major decisions that have influenced Romanian education in the past decade. Agents currently controlling the focus of change and the future challenges facing the Romanian educational system will both be considered.

The conceptual framework

Our analysis starts from the premise that the evolution of education reform in Romania does not reflect a clear linear internal logic. The complexity of the task of education reform has meant that the process of change has been neither completely controlled nor predictable; thus, a definitive model of change remains elusive. As Fullan (1999, p. 21) remarks: 'It is a theoretical and empirical impossibility to generate a theory that applies to all situations … [Although] theories of change can guide thinking and action … the reality of complexity tells us that each situation will have degrees of uniqueness in its history and makeup which will cause unpredictable differences to emerge.' Yet, the need to accumulate wisdom and experience about how the change process evolves is more acute than ever so that conditions which promote successful change can be considered and used to our advantage.

We begin our inquiry with an examination of some of the major decisions taken in the field of education since Romania broke from Communist rule in December 1989. The questions that form the basis of our inquiry include: How can the multitude of decisions that have had an impact on Romanian education be understood?

What mechanisms of change are evident? How quickly has change proceeded? Is there a clear direction indicated by the reform measures? Is this direction linked to reforms in other sectors of society? To what extent have we met the general objectives set by our educational policies? What are the major obstacles still to be overcome? Although not all these questions will receive equal in-depth examination, we hope that the following critical overview will afford the reader a clearer sense of the milestones in the reform of the Romanian education system post-1989.

The point of departure in our examination of Romania's education system is a framework of change which applies both the valuable insights provided by Fullan's model (2001) and the transition concepts developed by Bîrzea (1994). Although Fullan (1999) admits that the process of change is too complex to be captured in a single model, we have been able to outline a schema upon which we elaborate a conceptual framework for the analysis of both the process and the content of change in Romania. Fullan's framework (2001) postulates three interdependent phases: *initiation*, *implementation*, and *institutionalization*.

- Initiation consists of the process leading up to and including a decision to adopt or proceed with a change.
- Implementation or initial use involves the first experiences of putting an innovation into practice.
- Institutionalization (sometimes also called incorporation, generalization, routinization, or continuation) refers to whether the change gets built in as an ongoing part of the system or disappears by way of a decision or for lack of adequate resources (both financial and human).

We have identified four distinct phases governing the reform process in the Romanian educational system, which correspond to the stages of Fullan's conceptual framework: (a) deconstruction (corrective reform), (b) stabilization (reforms of modernization), (c) transformation (structural reforms), and (d) coordination (systemic reforms).

The *deconstruction* phase reflects the acknowledgement of the need for change. Starting with the 'decision to decide', the implementation of real change is not possible without a rethinking of the values, interests, and resources embodied in the current government policies and strategies. In this stage, the focus is limited to the correction and replacement of existing policies; what is deemed obsolete, limited, or inadequate is removed on the basis of reinterpreted values, new emergent interests, or revised use of existing resources. Change at this stage is typically *ad hoc* and implemented without consideration of systemic needs, or coherent understanding of the transformation process as a whole. Under such conditions, the routinization (institutionalization) stage cannot be reached.

The *stabilization* phase comprises all actions which stabilize the system and legitimise the changes made. In this stage, the procedural dynamics of policy formation come into play: decision-makers explore change from an exclusively technical perspective. Attempts to put innovations into practice are often fragmented, and routinization, as before, cannot be achieved. The basic structures of the system at this stage are untouched by the reform measures.

In agreement with Bryan D. Jones' decision matrix, introduced in *Politics and the Architecture of Choice* (2001, p. 44), we maintain that effective decision-making requires the difficult task of isolating all relevant attributes of a problem and comparing the solutions on all attributes. In Romania, only during the third stage, *transformation*, were efforts made to approach education reform in this way and to apply the analysis to the system as a whole. Once structural reforms are implemented, change becomes an ongoing part of the system; and, for the first time in the reform process, real institutionalization becomes possible.

However, one key element is still missing – the link between the education system and the broader environment. In our model, *coordination* refers to the phase in which the forces of change in education are combined, balanced, and related to those emerging in the political, economic, and administrative systems. Such systemic reform is the most difficult to achieve. As with most structural reforms, foreign input is an essential condition for its success.[1]

Over the past decade, change in the Romanian education system has taken place amidst tensions, multiple crises, and radical structural transformations in the public sector. Deregulation, privatization, and the transition to a free market generated uncertainty and destabilization. In Figure 6, we present our model and the key successive phases leading to the full-scale synergic transformation of the system.

'Deciding to decide'

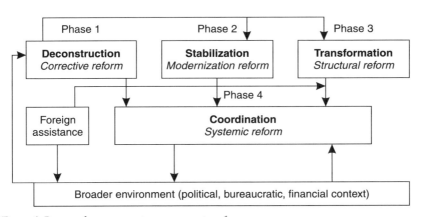

Figure 6 Passage from corrective to systemic reform.

---

1 In Romania, the promoters of change, as highlighted by several policy analysts, ignored the link between the education system and the broader environment. Only in the late 1990s did the new policies attempt to address the larger economic, social and political context and its impact on education (OECD, 2000).

Institutionalization of change

The model presented in Figure 6 may prove very useful, as it sets in order the major stages of educational change experienced by Romania during the last decade. It draws attention to some elements/assumptions that educational policy experts of the mid-1990s failed to consider: (a) transformation of an education system is a time-consuming endeavour: change is a gradual process in which every legislative milestone and corrective reform may be decisive; (b) external factors, such as international assistance, is very important to the success or fail-ure of educational policies; and (c) the social, political, and economic contexts in which the education system develops are vital factors in any attempt at systemic reform.

In Romania, the process of reform – starting with the 'decision to decide' and continuing through the institutionalization of systemic change – was extremely problematic, characterized by contradictions, regressive tendencies, and lack of real political support. The arrows in Figure 6 emphasize the interdependence of the various phases of our model, the effect of external assistance on educational policies, and the relationship of the various change initiatives to the broader political, social, and economic environment.

During the early years of educational reform, priorities were primarily external, the most important of which was the elimination of the deep-rooted Communist influences. The system was oversized and supported by limited resources;[2] there was a lack of alternative and intercultural education, excessive centralization and manifest political propaganda in the schools; the emphasis was on paramili-tary training, uniformity and annihilation of student individuality/autonomy, etc. Secondly, reform priorities focused on stabilizing the education system i.e. reducing compulsory education from ten to eight grades, removing the examina-tion from upper secondary school to midway to graduation, reducing class size and teaching loads, ensuring university autonomy while discarding polytechnic education as the foundation of educational policy.[3] However, many of these early initiatives (even some of which proved successful), lacked grounding in any information or diagnostic data base. Only during the second half of the 1990s, when the Ministry of National Education enlisted the assistance of inter-national bodies (such as the World Bank, the European Union, and the Open Society Fund), did system objectives became clear and a specific implementation strategy emerge. For the first time – in accordance with terms of reference and

---

2   The GDP share allocated to education was constantly decreasing: 3.5 per cent in 1975 and 2.1 per cent in 1985. In 1987, the expenditure per student was below US$200.
3   Many of these reforms were included in the Government Ordinance (May 1990), that became the first important piece of legislation adopted in the field of education after the fall of Communism.

priorities set by the funding programmes – structural reform began to be implemented in Romania.

It should be noted that the applicability of our model to the concrete realities of a country in transition is a measure of its validity across various socio-political contexts of change, including the atypical and chaotic. This case study will offer some insight into that process so that we can better define the challenges ahead. These challenges will surely include finding ways to increase public participation in decision-making and to involve all stakeholders in order to ensure successful implementation of decisions.

Using changing forces: acquaintance with complexity

Phase 1: corrective reforms: self-induced change (1990)

In the early 1960s, Romania's Communist government began to assert some independence from the Soviet Union. Nicolae Ceauşescu became head of the Communist Party in 1965 and head of state in 1967. Ceauşescu's denunciation of the 1968 Soviet invasion of Czechoslovakia and brief relaxation of internal repression helped give him a positive image both at home and in the West. Seduced by Ceauşescu's 'independent' foreign policy, Western leaders were slow to turn against a regime which, by the late 1970s, had become increasingly harsh, arbitrary, and capricious. Rapid economic growth, fuelled by foreign credit, gradually gave way to wrenching austerity and severe political repression. The dictatorship of the Ceauşescu family – considered to be one of the most absurd forms of totalitarianism in the 20th century – precipitated distortions in the economy, degradation of Romanian social and moral life, and increasing isolation from the international community. Ceauşescu, in his obsession with preposterously huge building projects, abused the country's resources; this resulted in a dramatic decline in the Romanian standard of living, and catapulted the nation into deepening social crisis.

The fall of Ceauşescu's regime took place midway through the 1989–1990 school year, causing major disruption of the education system. The spark of revolt ignited in Timisoara on December 16, 1989 rapidly spread throughout the country, and on December 22 the dictatorship was overthrown in a bloody coup. The victory of the revolution created a window of opportunity for the re-establishment of a democratic, pluralistic political system, a return to a free market economy, and a reintegration of the country into the European economic, political, and cultural space.[4] Destabilization was the price that Romanian society paid for the destruction of an intensely oppressive and inflexible system.

---

4 At the November 2002 Summit in Prague, the North Atlantic Treaty Organization (NATO) leaders invited Romania to join the alliance. In addition, in 2007 Romania will become a member of the European Union.

Adopted in May 1990 by a government ordinance, the first education-reform measures were intended to lend a modicum of coherence to some changes which had occurred spontaneously – a *de jure* confirmation of *de facto* changes (Bîrzea, 1996). Throughout the transition process, many voices were raised against decision-makers – particularly those who, in 1990, first instigated education reform – for failing to recognize the West (with its vast and lengthy experience in education reform) as a great potential resource.

As regularization of the education system proceeded, many measures were implemented which closely reflected the interests of all stakeholders (students, professors, directors, parents, etc.). The most significant changes undertaken during the 1990–1991 school year involved reducing the number of years of compulsory education from ten to eight (reflecting a shift in emphasis from quantity to quality); discarding polytechnic education as the foundation of educational policies; ensuring university autonomy; eliminating the meaningless examinations which were formally held half-way through studies; limiting class size (to 36 students per class); decreasing teaching load (from 22 to 18 classes per week in urban areas, 16 classes per week in rural areas); and guaranteeing education in the languages of ethnic minorities.

Of equally great significance were the measures which ultimately led to the institutionalization of reforms important to further development of the system. These include the expansion of the general (academic) secondary school system (in 1989, these excellent traditional schools represented only 5 per cent of secondary institutions; this increased to 40 per cent by 1992); the diversification of secondary education with new fields and subjects; the provision of intensive foreign language training; the introduction of post-secondary schools offering two or three years of training; and the inclusion of subjects in the curriculum which encourage critical thinking and synthesis, e.g. philosophy, psychology, sociology and civic education. In general, these measures corresponded to those adopted for the modernization of education systems worldwide; consequently, Romania's need to design and test corrective policies was greatly reduced.

According to Fullan (2001), there are four elements essential to the success of change projects: strong advocacy, perceived need, active initiation, and a clear model for proceeding. In Romania, no needs-assessment or model for proceeding existed; rather, initial changes in the system took place almost spontaneously. However, after so many years of under-funding and marginalization of education, there was strong community support for change. Such consensus was instrumental in abolishing Communist education's most egregious features; however, by the early 1990s, the government still failed to define a new policy framework for the reform of Romanian education.

The first stage of reform merely entailed minor operational decisions (OECD, 2000). It was only in the next stage that decision-makers began to create a framework for strategic planning and for defining national policy. They were obliged to face the reality that current problems had been caused in part by the failure of educational analysts to recognize the highly complex economic context of educational reform and the impact of concurrent social and political changes.

Phase 2: modernization policies – discovering the forces of change (1991–1992)

Before reconstruction of an education system deeply affected by the political changes of 1989 could begin, it was necessary to create a stabilizing climate. To that end, the government ordinance of May 1990 (issued by Government Decision No. 461/1991) implemented a number of new measures, including the introduction of three consecutive cycles and the establishment of selective admission procedures for higher education; the resumption of special-education management by the Ministry of National Education; and the introduction of alternative schools and pedagogical models in the school system (e.g. Freinet, Montessori, Waldorf, and Peterse).

In the 1990s, Romania, like all former-Communist societies, struggled to maintain the operation of its institutions as they underwent a process of profound change. Important decisions had to be made 'on the spot', with no time available for elaboration, evaluation, or the formulation of a vision. Adrian Miroiu (1998, 2000) has characterized this as a period in which the post-Communist state was, paradoxically, both vehicle for reform and object of reform; even as the state conferred legality on new institutions and social regulations, it was itself becoming increasingly de-legitimized (Miroiu, 2000). Elster (1993) compares the decision-makers in transition countries to 'a crew facing the task of rebuilding a boat in the open sea'.

In the absence of a Law on Education,[5] the new Constitution (enacted in December 1991) represented a significant step towards the establishment of a legal foundation for education. The Constitution stipulates the basic tenets of Romanian education: freedom of access, new structure reform, diversification of programmes, high quality education, choice of language of instruction, autonomy of higher education, openness towards private education, and provision of alternative schools.

However, serious challenges remained. For those engaged in education reform, applied analyses are a valuable source of information about such matters as cost-benefit ratios, the compatibility of decisions with those made in other sectors, the unintended effects of reform measures, etc. In Romania, decisions made without benefit of such resources often had detrimental consequences. This stage is characterized by trust and optimism in the government's ability to transform reality according to pursued targets; however, although various educational policies were developed, an optimal solution to Romania's educational crisis was yet to be found. A full picture of the complexities of the educational system emerged only

---

5   The Communist Law in Education (1978) had not been formally repealed.

after the various policies stumbled on their way toward institutionalization. The forces of change had been put to work; yet the failures demonstrated that they could not be entirely *controlled* – discrediting the naïve belief that knowing *what* to do means knowing *how* to do it. The most important issues which crystallized at the end of this second stage included the absence of a comprehensive diagnosis of the Romanian education system, a lack of knowledge of reform alternatives, limited competence in managing change, crisis in the in-service teacher training programme, and difficulty in mobilizing educators to support the change efforts of the ministry. In addition, the system had preserved an excessively central-ized decision-making system with insufficient and/or poorly managed financial resources, making change even more difficult.

A crucial decision was made: to seek public input and advice regarding chang-es in education. In the early 1990s an open debate on the Law on Education was launched. Over 2000 amendments were submitted by key stakeholders (teachers, parents, NGOs), and numerous alternative projects were prepared by the par-liamentary opposition. Although the latter hampered the ratification of the law and caused contentious political interests to surface, such public participation represented Romania's first examples of democratization of the decision-making process. The benefits of these efforts to enlist the public became apparent in the next stage of educational change, namely, structural reform.

Phase 3: structural reforms – successes and failures in the initiation of change (1993–1996)

Notwithstanding a stagnant economy,[6] Romania began restructuring its educa-tion system by 1993. This third stage of educational reform brought about the realization that the real change could not be achieved by means of Ministry of National Education directives to county school inspectorates: it would require a profound reformation of structures themselves, i.e. involvement of the entire organization and operation of the education system.

In 1993–1994, the first structural reforms made with full recognition of the changing forces governing education were introduced and implementation began. Early approaches to restructuring may have had limited success; nevertheless, it was during this time that Romania's first national education policy documents were prepared. These documents included: *Education Reform in Romania*, drafted by an expert team from the Institute of Education Sciences (1993); *Higher Educa-tion Reform in Romania*, prepared by the Consultative Group for Higher Education and Research (1994); and *The White Book of the Reform of Education in Romania* (1995) published by the Ministry of National Education. For the first time since 1989, comprehensive reforms materialized in Romanian educational policy: de-mocratization of the education system (openness, flexibility, and decentralization);

6 Privatization proceeded slowly, although it began to pick up in 1997.

improved quality of education (increased internal and external efficiency); as well, there was a growing recognition of the importance of linking educational reforms to government national human resource strategies. For the first time, issues of financing and infrastructure received in-depth analysis and were included in comprehensive programmes.[7] The government also took important steps to ensure that proposals were implemented, i.e. led to real changes.

In 1995, the Law on Education was finally adopted, making possible the comprehensive restructuring of Romania's education system: not only its goals and objectives but also its administrative structures, curricula, textbooks, evaluation tools, and in-service teacher training system. These changes were considered part of a long-term process; the new agenda forced the administration, in order to diminish the gap between intention and achievement, to improve its capacity to manage education reform. At this point, *foreign assistance* became the main force pushing reforms forward. External joint financing was one of the priorities of this stage: the government realized that restructuring could not be accomplished with internal (human and material) resources alone.

In the third phase, Romania's major partners in the reform of its education system were the World Bank and the European Union. Each donor created its own institutional system to administer its projects, which were financed only for the term of the partnership contract. World Bank projects established national boards for designing new curricula, alternative school books, teacher training, evaluation and assessment, occupational standards, educational management and financing; the VET PHARE programme financed a variety of pilot and demonstration schools. The three- to four-year duration of these programmes corresponds to the reference period of the 'implementation' stage of Fullan's conceptual framework.

Other major projects which received financial support from the World Bank included pre-university education (US$55 million); higher education and scientific research (US$25 million); and vocational counselling and career information (US$10 million). The World Bank loan was conditional, focused upon precise objectives, and necessarily linked to the new reform directives. Preparations were initiated for changing all pre-university syllabi, and the system of state-controlled textbooks was abandoned, leading the way to liberalization of the pedagogical market. New curricula were developed; religious instruction, for example, was introduced into the teaching plan: compulsory in primary education, optional in gymnasia, and an elective in high schools and vocational education. New module programmes were designed. The in-service teacher training system was

---

7   However, only after the mid-1990s were concrete programmes (e.g. rehabilitation of schools, development of rural education) initiated. Even though this phase witnessed a continuous increase of budget allocations for education, a portion of these resources was withdrawn from the education budget and reallocated to the repayment of the foreign debt. Yet, low government funding for maintenance and improvement of the educational infrastructure, acquisition of new materials and equipment, and improvement of teacher salaries hindered but did not arrest the drive for comprehensive educational reform.

re-examined and the evaluation and examination system reviewed. This latter reform denoted a shift in emphasis from 'quantity' (based on number of compulsory studies) to 'quality' (based on effectiveness of teaching and learning); the introduction of a mechanism, based on public reports, for annual evaluation of the education system; the development of national standards for all subjects and education levels; and the development of an institutional framework for evaluation.

In 1995, the EU, through its PHARE programme, offered important support (€125 million), specifically targeting vocational education, a dynamic component of Romania's educational system. Relevant objectives were negotiated with Romanian authorities: the development of new vocational curricula, the design of innovative teaching and learning materials in vocational schools, the updating of training requirements for teachers and master instructors (including managerial training for principals), the introduction of professional standards and qualifications better suited to a market economy,[8] and the improvement and modernization of professional training equipment. Additional resources came from other EU programmes, including TEMPUS, SOCRATES, LEONARDO, and Youth for Europe.

The goals and objectives of Romania's education system had changed; however, much remained to be done in reforming the administrative structures, curricula, textbooks, evaluation tools, and in-service teacher-training system. The Law on Education had established a clear set of principles: the definition of education as a national priority; the end of excessive state control; guaranteed free access for all social, ethnic, cultural, and linguistic groups; and the provision of instruction to students with special needs.

Yet the Romanian educational system was dependent on a society which itself had attained only partial transformation on its way to modernization – a society whose labour-force was overwhelmingly pre-industrial, whose service industry was underdeveloped, whose population was becoming increasingly rural, and whose middle class, in socio-economic terms, was insignificant. All of these considerations forced a re-evaluation of the nation's education-reform plans. Poverty was growing; the poor, women, and minority groups swelled the ranks of the excluded and marginalized. Decision-makers in education were taught a new lesson by the forces of change: *educational reform had to be coordinated with reform in other sectors of society*; otherwise, major change would be unsustainable and impossible to institutionalize.

As mentioned earlier, important initiatives at all education levels helped create a certain balance. However, as Miroiu (1998) notes, this balance was a delicate one. On the one hand were changes which already were under way, with strong pressure to continue with the momentum of change. On the other hand were the conservative forces which held back education reform, hindering the system's

---

8 This objective was initiated and coordinated by the World Bank, whereby alternative work standards were designed through a new cooperation between state, employer, and union.

preparations for substantive changes taking place in other sections of Romanian society. In addition, reform had been neglected in several areas, with unfortunate consequences: rural schools suffered from low enrolments, inadequate facilities, a dearth of qualified teachers, and high drop-out rates; minority-group education was still fraught with problems of equal educational access and opportunity, education in the mother tongue, and curricula insensitive to minority culture, values, and traditions.

Phase 4: the continuation of structural changes – in search of systemic reform (1996–2000)

In 1996, following Romania's first democratic elections, the Ministry of National Education appointed a new team to lead education reform. Making extensive use of foreign assistance (through twinning projects, transfer of know-how, and co-management), these authorities produced a document called *The Model of Romania's Rebirth through Education*, which pointed to education as the force able to trigger the mechanisms critical to the modernization of society at large. Education was now recognized as a *national priority*, essential for training Romanian's citizens to live and work in a democratic society. The government's new vision represents a new phase of policy development: according to the model in Figure 6, Romania has now entered the phase of *systemic reforms*. The newly appointed team pursued many reforms initiated by the previous team; but most importantly, they tried to link education to reforms initiated in *other* fields (the labour market, rural development, social assistance, etc.). These measures (adopted over the course of four years of democratic government [1996–2000] and integrated into the diverse development-policy documents)[9] constituted the first steps toward systemic reform.

In December 1997, Andrei Marga,[10] the Minister of National Education, made a statement expressing the Ministry's fervent commitment to comprehensive and sustained reform: schools were to become sources of moral, cognitive, and technological innovation for the whole society; school structures, outcomes, and administration were to be brought up to European standards. The point of departure for the Ministry of National Education's new reform team was a twofold question: 'What can society do for schools, and what can schools do for society?'

However, the disappointing performance of Romanian students at the *Third International Mathematics and Science Survey* (TIMSS) (Noveanu, 2001) revealed a decline in subject areas which, until then, had been considered strengths of the Romanian education system. Out of 41 participating countries, Romania ranked 31st in science and 34th in math; the successes of several Olympiad champions were overshadowed by this dismal showing. Neighbouring

9 The most important of such documents was the government's National Plan for Development.
10 As cited in Marga, 1998.

Central and Eastern European countries fared better: in science and math respectively, the Czech Republic finished 2nd and 6th, Hungary ranked 9th and 14th, and Bulgaria was placed 5th and 11th. The survey results shocked Romania; there were many who did not trust them. The TIMSS standings signalled the urgency of pushing forward certain initiatives (e.g. a generalized curriculum); the survey acutely focused attention on the need to evaluate the efficiency of the Romanian education system and the necessity of meeting international standards (OECD, 1999). Once again, foreign assistance proved decisive in addressing these needs. Romanian decision-makers were well aware of the World Bank's 'comprehensive reform' initiative and its clearly-defined objectives: redefinition of the central functions of higher education (problem-solving, innovation, and university research); development of infrastructure necessary for linking institutions to national and international communication systems; decentralization of school and university management; greater institutional autonomy; progress towards a global financing system (to be promoted by granting educational institutions greater freedom in financial decision-making); and the establishment, based on performance and operational compatibility criteria, of joint curriculum and research units. While continuing to assist with ongoing programmes (e.g. curricular changes, restructuring of pre-academic and academic institutions, revitalizing university scientific research, etc.), the World Bank initiated new projects designed to improve educational infrastructure, school management, and rural education. According to a study of the Romanian education system (Miroiu, 1998), all programmes sought to eliminate the polarization between social norms imbued with egocentrism, elitism, intellectualism, and authoritarianism and the ideals of the education system. Two examples merit attention.

The successes of the European Union-financed vocational education programme resulted in its application to the entire Romanian VET system in the 1999/2000 school year. The decision to implement this programme nation-wide was based on a final evaluation conducted by the European Training Foundation. The following year saw the implementation of a new high-school curriculum based on the same principles as the PHARE programme for the technological stream.

The Open Society Foundation provided notable support. It financed an in-depth evaluation of rural education to identify both current problems and long-term improvement strategies (Jigău, 2001). As well, the Ministry of National Education initiated programmes for young and older dropouts in cooperation with Education 2000+, a member of the Open Society Foundation network (*Second Chance Program*); this was one of the first major joint ventures of a central public authority and a non-governmental organization in education.

Lessons to be learned

Loasby (1999, p. 130) asserts that 'a knowledge-rich society must be an ecology of specialists. And since knowledge is distributed within each human brain, organisation, and within the economic and social system, it could grow, provided that it is sufficiently coordinated to support increasing interdependencies'. In retrospect, it may be said that Romania's experience in the 1990s was different from other post-Communist countries in transition in two ways:

- Education reform was ahead of economic reform.
- Romania garnered the largest amount of foreign support for educational reform among East European countries.

These achievements may seem surprising if we consider Romania's general evolution from an economic and social standpoint. On the one hand, Romanian economic reform was a rather slow and winding process, marked by a constant degradation of the standard of living. Educational reform, although lacking solid support from the economic sector, was more daring, quickly attaining two goals not yet reached by economic reform, i.e. *decentralization* and *liberalization* of the educational market. On the other hand, foreign investment was much more substantial in education than in the economic sector. Compared to other countries in transition, Romania assumed the majority of World Bank education projects, and benefited from important European Union and Open Society funds in addition to bilateral sources.

However, the aforementioned distinctions demand more careful analysis; precisely these two apparent achievements may prove to be factors of constraint. Educational reform has indeed outrun economic reform; but it is exactly this lead that has given rise to most of the current problems, e.g. the impossibility of generalizing innovations, the inability to absorb external programmes, and the insufficient allocation of human resources to the process of development. It is also true that education benefited from considerable external funding. Yet, in the absence of a coherent policy and adequate internal support, external contributions failed to yield anticipated results. The case of Romani (minority) education offers an illustration of some of these problems. After many years in which this issue was conspicuously absent from official policy documents, international organizations and Romani and non-Romani NGOs persuaded the Ministry of National Education to provide Romani children with equal opportunity and schooling and to promote Romani identity through the education process. As a first step, the government undertook general measures relevant to all Romanian minority groups: drawing up new textbooks dealing with the history and cultural traditions of Romania's minorities; ensuring minority group representation among school leaders and specialists; and promoting educational diversity and dialogue (for example, by initiating a programme for translating school books from Romanian to other ethnic languages). Following these general initiatives, a second round of measures specifically addressed Romani needs; these included the creation of new institutional structures, the introduction of Romani in schools as a heritage language, and the development of a new syllabus and selected curricular instruments for Romani students. A special Department of Romani Language has been established at Bucharest University and several Romani textbooks have been published. Yet these reforms, for all their progressiveness, remain far from being systematized. One reason for this is the scarcity of instructors – there are few Romani teachers and most lack proper qualifications; another explanation is the lack of coordination between various initiatives: new policies allowing schools to design and develop 30 per cent of the broader (school-based) curriculum failed to consider the specific values, traditions, and needs of this ethnic group. Many obstacles still remain to eliminating discrimination and ensuring equal opportunity for Romani students. The absence of identification cards is still a pretext for excluding Romani children from the public school system. As Horvath and Scacco have noted (2001, p. 271), innovative solutions to the challenges of Romani education (such as mobile 'caravan schools' compatible with the semi-nomadic lifestyle of the Romani population) are not encouraged; what is more, the positive models provided by NGO-promoted educational projects have failed, so far, to inspire policy development in the area of minority education.

Once again, it must be emphasized that the input of international bodies was decisive for the initiation and implementation of major reforms.[11] However, in the institutionalization stages, international assistance has been *decreasing* while the role of all levels of government (national, regional, and local) is becoming increasingly critical. It is quite possible that these tendencies have appeared in other transition countries as well; in the 1990s, these countries' significant but unsustainable investments in education produced only modest effects. The application of our model to the specific example of Romania in the last decade may help illuminate the forces that affect educational change in countries in transition.

Romanians today express diminishing confidence in the quality of their education and their ability to find employment. In some transition countries such as Romania, intellectuals (including teachers) are very poorly paid and must struggle to survive. In such circumstances, more families, especially the well-to-do, lose faith in the value of degrees and qualifications. Conversely, family attitudes towards education are themselves a major determinant of school attendance and student outcomes. One way to restore faith in the school system is to involve the family early on in the educational process. Of course, the success of such a strategy depends on the quality of teaching and the openess of the teaching staff. In a recent opinion poll,[12] 10 per cent of respondents considered education the most important problem currently facing their country. And although citizens express low levels of confidence in educators, their levels of confidence in other professions is even lower. The greatest challenge facing the Romanian education system may be to put lessons of international assistance to best use to ensure sustainability of major programmes. One of

---

11 Following the model described in Figure 6 earlier in this chapter, foreign assistance may take the form of financial resources and/or know-how, and may have bearing on all stages of the policy chain, from design to evaluation and correction.

12 This poll was part of a regional study conducted in Romania by the Centre for Economic Development (Vitosa Research, 2001).

the most important lessons is that communication between parents, educators, administrators, and local and national communities is critical (OECD, 2000).

Concluding remarks

Our discussion of Romania's four stages of educational reform revealed that moves from structural to systemic policies should be painstakingly researched and thoroughly planned. Premature visions may be tantamount to blind planning. In terms of our model, Romania's education system at the present time exhibits three key features: lack of cohesion among programmes launched by various donors; dependence on external sources of financing; and rejection of innovation as a result of lack of readiness (as in the case of alternative textbooks which teachers had not been trained to use).

In the absence of a clear policy for integrating foreign-assistance programmes, the majority of implementation activities depend upon *temporary structures* created with foreign financing within these programmes. Even more alarming is the fact that all three major donors (World Bank, the European Union, and the Open Society) promote different educational philosophies, which are at times difficult to reconcile:

- *Structural adjustment* (World Bank) emphasizes market mechanisms (alternative school books, external evaluation, free and competitive production of teaching aids). In a context where the market is fragile and the State in decline, the liberalization of the educational market is a solution of limited effectiveness.
- *Accession policy* grants priority to institutions that favour the achievement of *acquis communitaire* (harmonization of Romanian legislation with that of the European Union). According to the principle of subsidiarity, education and training are national competencies; thus, community support is limited to issues related to the common European market (workforce mobility, mutual recognition of qualifications, increase in competitiveness).
- *Open Society* (Open Society Foundation) primarily supports educational alternatives, bottom-up reform, and the development of civil society.

To integrate three such different approaches into a coherent policy is an intricate task, made more arduous by a lack of adequate financial support from the State. The moment the respective programmes were launched, the State moved to set up two conditions:

- internal financing (a minimum of 30 per cent of total project costs); and
- continuation structures to take over the respective activities, once the foreign presence recedes.

Since 85 per cent of the education budget is allocated to salaries, little remains for innovation and development. For their part, local communities and non-profit organizations have other priorities, and their involvement in education support is minimal. The education system's dependence on external and on ever-dwindling State resources creates problems in moving from implementation to institutionalization. Most countries in transition – obliged to carry out radical reforms in times of austerity and economic decline – likely find themselves in a similar situation.

Various analyses of Romanian education have identified the following as critical issues which must urgently be addressed:

- Many top-level and intermediate administrative bodies are ahead of local educational structures; thus, there is a need to generate capacity-building at this grass-roots level in order to promote local involvement in the reform process;
- Key county institutions (inspectorates, teacher staff centres, universities, and schools) experience difficulty in the implementation of reforms;
- Teacher education must be constantly re-evaluated and improved; and
- There is a need for more community involvement and school-based approaches to education.

According to national statistics, the economic situation in Romania began to improve in the first part of 2001. It is projected that this positive trend (attributable both to economic reforms of the late 1990s and to economic discipline and the encouragement of investment in 2001) will continue into 2004. Such a propitious context is expected to give fresh impetus to investment in human resources. Accordingly, the institutionalization stage of education reform – although delayed somewhat relative to the implementation stage (1994–2000) – was re-launched in the 2001/2002 school year. Favourable economic and political conditions should not only encourage more internal spending on education, but also attract new external resources; indeed, the European Union has already launched (2001) new priority programmes for development of rural education, large-scale introduction of ICT (information communication and technology) and e-Learning, and improvement of Romani education. The year 2000 began on an auspicious note, as well: after the Helsinki summit (December 1999), Romania was invited to begin the process of application for EU membership;[13] such status would, no doubt, bring not only external pressure to accelerate economic reform but also an influx of financial resources. In addition, important policy documents, e.g. the Governing Plan (2001–2004) and the 'National Employment Plan' (2000) have accorded a new primacy to human resource development. Recognizing the crucial role of education reform in sustainable development, they have placed education and training in the centre of sector-based policies and have established new priorities. This new orientation encourages optimism about overcoming current problems in the move from implementation to institutionalization. However, special attention must be given to designing strategies that will ensure *equal access* for the

13 See footnote 4.

most disadvantaged groups in Romanian society. As Adam Swift (2001, p. 116) argues, access to and level of educational attainment are decisive in determining one's success and status in the labour market. Since the restriction of access to particular forms of education has always served as a dominant form of social exclusion, it is critical that, irrespective of class or wealth, all learners have the opportunity to benefit from programmes. Jigău (2001, p. 30), in a recent in-depth study of Romanian rural education,[14] offers several examples of disparities which still affect the Romanian educational system, e.g. unequal access to education, limited opportunities for multiple career choices based on different skill and competency levels, and uneven student/school performance outcomes.

As promoted by the Ministry of Education after the November 2000 elections, the priorities of the new stage of *systemic reform* are to ensure the quality of education (mainly by raising standards); to reduce the drop-out rate (about 17 per cent of the students drop out before grade 9); to provide ICT support for education; and to transform the teacher-training (especially in-service) system.

Despite structural reforms, low external efficiency of the educational system is already apparent: according to official statistics, in 1999 over 40 per cent of the unemployed were high school graduates; as a result, the development of adult education and continuing vocational training have become a new educational priority. This situation demonstrates the need (emphasized in our model) for educational policies to pay closer attention to the relationship between schools and the economic environment.

Education development clusters, an interesting new trend at the regional level, may hold promise as exemplars of greater congruence between education and economy. Resources and projects are grouped together, usually around major universities and the Institute of Education Sciences. Participants include academic and professional researchers as well as local school inspectors, principals, adult educators, parents, representatives of 'school houses' (local centres for in-service teacher training), and NGOs. Ad-hoc regrouping of resources and institutions may take place to allow participation in development programmes financed by PHARE, Open Society, the World Bank, and/or the government. The system is extremely dynamic, succeeding both in encouraging local initiative and in bringing together the most diverse of partners on a joint project. It represents a successful linking of the education system and the economic environment: just as the education system depends on the economy for financing, the economy needs school graduates whose attitudes and abilities promote employee productivity and managerial competency (OECD, 2000). This link between economy and education is definitely acknowledged by the Romanian government and has been included in its education reform agenda.

Our current educational objectives can be reached through public programmes monitored by the Ministry of Education and Research, and financed with public

---

14 This study was based on an investigation of more than 19,000 school units, representing approximately 95% of the total number of school units existing in rural areas in Romania.

resources and state-guaranteed loans provided by such entities as the World Bank. As accession processes advance, the main support for education-reform programmes will no longer be provided by the World Bank but by the European Union. Complementary to these top-down and *state-controlled programmes* are numerous *grass-root projects* initiated by schools and by civil society. These projects, which focus on programmes such as alternative education, education for democratic citizenship, school-community partnerships, non-formal learning, youth participation, and education for the Romani minority, could represent an important contribution to the current reform movement.[15] Given the current success of these spontaneous, locally initiated programmes, institutionalization should have been ensured not only by the Romanian partner who is required to co-finance the programme from the very moment it is launched (at a minimum 30 per cent of the total cost), but also by the timely establishment of follow-up structures to *take over* the activities and spread them throughout the educational system, once the foreign presence recedes. Failure to include these considerations could vitiate the steps taken thus far to transform the education system and thwart Romania's evolution toward systemic reform. We must learn the lessons of our past failures before we can move forward. If we do so, there is a chance that values and principles will replace opportunism and that policy processes will be driven by moral purpose rather than political expediency. Then, as imagined by Swift (2001), those who are most adept at translating abstract ideas into concrete policies may become the key agents of genuine change.

References

Bîrzea, C. (1994) *Educational Policies of the Countries in Transition*. Strasbourg: The Council of Europe Press.

Bîrzea, C. (1996) The dilemmas of the reform of Romanian education: shock therapy, the infusion of innovation, or cultural de-communisation? *Higher Education in Europe*, 22(3), 321–327.

Carothers, T. (1999) *Aiding Democracy Abroad: The Learning Curve*. Washington: Carnegie Endowment for International Peace.

Elster, J. (1993) Constitution making in Eastern Europe: rebuilding the boat in the open sea. In J. Hesse (Ed.), *Administrative Transformation in Central and Eastern Europe: Towards Public Sector Reform in Post-Communist Societies* (pp. 169–217). Oxford: Blackwell.

Fullan, M. (1999) *Change Forces: The Sequel*. London: The Falmer Press.

Fullan, M. (2001) *The New Meaning of Education Change* (3rd edn). New York: Teachers College Press.

15 According to *Romania – Country Strategy Paper* (London Department for International Development, 1999), this view is shared by most local offices of international organizations that are active in Romanian education.

Government of Romania (2000) *Governing Plan* (2001–2004). Bucharest, retrieved March 15, 2003 from <http://www.gv.ro/obiective/programguv/pgguv.pdf>

Government of Romania (2002) *National Employment Plan*, Ministry of Labor and Social Solidarity, Bucharest. Retrieved March 15, 2003 from <http://www.mmss.ro//programe.htm>

Horvath, I. and Scacco, A. (2001) From the unitary to the pluralistic: fine tuning minority policy in Romania. In A. Biro and P. Kovacs (Eds), *Diversity in Action, Local Government and Public Service Reform Initiative* (pp. 241–273). Budapest: Open Society Institute.

Jones, B. D. (2001) *Politics and the Architecture of Choice: Bounded Rationality and Governance*. Chicago: University of Chicago Press.

Jigău M. (Coordinator) (2001) *Rural Education in Romania: Background, Difficulties and Development Strategies* (2nd edn). Bucharest: UNICEF, Ministry of National Education, Institute of Educational Sciences.

Loasby, B. J. (1999) *Knowledge, Institutions and Evolution in Economics*. London: Routledge Press.

London Department for International Development (1999) *Romania – Country Strategy Paper*: London: Department for International Development.

Marga, A. (1998) *Guidelines for the Reform of Education in Romania*. Bucharest: Ministry of National Education.

Miroiu, A. (Ed.) (1998) *Învăţământul Românesc Azi*. Bucharest: Editura Polirom.

Miroiu, A. (Ed.) (2000) *Reform of Public Sector in Romania*, Bucharest: Editura Trei.

Noveanu, G. (Ed.) (2001) *Third International Mathematics and Science Survey (TIMSS-R – National Report)*. Bucharest: Institute of Educational Sciences.

OECD (2000) *Review of National Policies for Education – Romania*. Paris: OECD.

Swift, A. (2001) *Political Philosophy*. Cambridge: Polity Press.

Vitosa Research (2001) *Corruption indexes, regional corruption monitoring in Albania, Bosnia & Herzegovina, Bulgaria, Croatia, Macedonia, Romania and Yugoslavia* – March 2000. Sofia: Vitosa Research.

6

EDUCATIONAL TRANSITION IN EAST GERMANY

Between emancipation and adjustment

Nina Arnhold, Project Leader, Centre for Higher Education Development, Germany

'Immediately, without delay!' That was the answer Günther Schabowski, member of the Politburo, gave in response to a journalist who asked when German Democratic Republic (GDR) citizens could profit from the new travel regulations just announced at the same press conference. Immediately following the announcement, thousands of East Berliners set off to prove its accuracy. The November 9, 1989 opening of the inner German border and the destruction of the Wall became the ultimate symbols of the dramatic changes which had already started to affect the GDR some months earlier. These events must be seen as a reaction to the mass demonstrations in Leipzig and other parts of the country: a concession to the demands of the people for freedom of the press, freedom to travel, and democratic elections.

However, the expected changes did not occur that suddenly. After Mikhail Gorbachev proclaimed the principles of *glasnost* and *perestroika,* an 'antiauthoritarian climate' (McLeish and Phillips, 1998) affected the countries of the Soviet Bloc. These countries had developed a set of common features as a result of a social order chosen (or more precisely, imposed) by and modelled after the Soviet Union. Following the dissolution of the Communist state, together these countries entered the 'valley of tears' (Dahrendorf, 1991): a period of political, economic, social, and cultural uncertainty accompanied by the search for a new identity. However, the gulf between these former 'allies' quickly broadened. Hungary, the Czech Republic, and Poland were in a position to pick up the threads of political and economic structures created in the post-war period (Bîrzea, 1994). As well, they were able to draw on a sense of national identity which had not been as severely impaired as that of certain other Communist states such as the GDR. Still other former Soviet republics 'left the track' by returning to some form of an authoritarian state.

The 'inter-regnum' period (Bîrzea, 1994, p. 18) – a period characterized by liberation from the most restrictive and oppressive aspects of the authoritarian system, a certain degree of experimentation and openness, and substantial uncertainty regarding the political outlook – lasted for less than one year in East Germany. After the demonstrations in autumn 1989 and the opening of the border to the West, the government was forced to resign and Communist hard-liners were replaced by soft-liners. The new government, under the leadership of Hans Modrow, attempted to introduce a reformed socialism while maintaining two German states, introducing a limited number of reforms and paving the way for the first democratic elections in the GDR in March 1990. The success of the Christian Democrats in these elections made it clear that the majority of East Germans rejected the concepts represented by the Modrow government and supported quick unification. The following months were dominated by preparations for unification. In July 1990, the D-Mark became the common currency of both East and West Germany, and in August the federal structure was re-introduced into the East. When in October 1990 the unification of the two German states became reality, it was obvious that this was not the growing-together of two equal partners but the extension of the political system of the Federal Republic of Germany (FRG) to the East.

This chapter sets out to describe some aspects of the transformation of the East German education system, primarily by citing examples from the school and higher-education systems and from research. A theoretical framework of transition, which is presented and elaborated below, will be used to analyse these changes.

Theoretical approach

O'Donnell and Schmitters (1986) define political transition as 'the interval between one political regime and another … delimited, on the one side, by the launching of the process of dissolution of an authoritarian regime and, on the other, by the installation of some form of democracy, the return to some form of authoritarian regime, or the emergence of a revolutionary alternative' (O'Donnell and Schmitters, 1986, p. 6). However, in recent years there has been a tendency to apply the term 'transition' mainly in cases of countries that have chosen democracy as their envisaged destination. In studying the literature on transition, one finds that some transition theories, in attempting to explain too much, remain so general as to be inapplicable to any concrete setting. Bîrzea (1994, p. 9) offers three reasons why it is nevertheless desirable to develop cogent theories of transition: (a) they help to understand an 'unprecedented historical phenomenon'; (b) they help in the development of more effective reform solutions for countries in transition; and (c) they enable Western countries to monitor the change processes (and offer assistance to) countries undergoing transitions for which they may – as Bîrzea stresses – be totally unprepared.

Bîrzea compares and contrasts the evolution of educational policy in a number of former Soviet-Bloc states by looking chiefly at three factors (Bîrzea, 1994, p. 8):

1   the initial state, i.e. the starting point of transition;
2   the destination, i.e. the objectives pursued; and
3   the actual content of transition, i.e. the derived transformations.

Bîrzea (1994) considers transition to be a 'set of interdependent economic, political and social reforms' (p. 12). Political reforms, i.e. constitutional reforms and the installation of political institutions and institutional features linked with the concept of civil society, are usually the first steps towards democracy. Subsequent economic and social reforms may take several years to effect; the attendant change of attitudes and values, even longer. Initially, there was a tendency to underestimate this cultural dimension of the transition process. However, in the 1990s, the widespread emergence of nostalgia in societies in transition has pointed to the very heart of the problem. As Bîrzea (1996) writes:

> ... the transitions in central and eastern Europe have turned out to be much more complicated than a simple moral or ideological victory. In general, analyses of this kind have focused exclusively on institutional transitions; that is, on setting up the three pillars of the new social order: political pluralism, the rule of law, and a market economy. These transformations, while significant, cannot stand alone. Cultural transition – the changing of mentalities, attitudes, values and social relations – is a more delicate matter. The institutional transition may last five to six years, whereas the cultural transition could take at least a generation.
> (Bîrzea, 1996, p. 674).

In a similar vein, Dahrendorf (1991) reminds us that the new political system must pass at least two 'turnover tests' (e.g. through political crisis) before the installation of democracy can be considered successful.

In 1995, a group of researchers from the Department of Educational Studies of the University of Oxford, through extensive analysis and discussion of Bîrzea's approach and by matching it with events and processes in countries as different as Latvia, East Germany, and South Africa, began to develop their own model of transition. First, these researchers examined the former education systems in each of these countries in terms of the incipient model, with a view to evaluating the utility of its emergent concepts. Next, they formulated the concept of educational transition in terms of a movement from certainty to uncertainty, from uniformity to diversity, from control to autonomy, etc. (McLeish and Phillips, 1998, p. 7). Soon a model emerged that:

depended not on a regular linear progression but on variable movement (in time terms) from one condition to another – much as the ripples caused by a stone dropped into a pool will produce an outwardly developing series of circles, their rate of development dependent on the force created by the initial impact of the stone. In the case of the group's model, the fall of the 'stone' is the collapse of the closed authoritarian system.

(McLeish and Phillips, 1998, p. 8)[1]

The model developed by this group of Oxford researchers is depicted in the middle column of Figure 7. It represents the authoritarian system as endangered by an anti-authoritarian climate that leads to ideological collapse. It is not easy to state exactly when this phase commenced in the GDR; however, the demonstrations of autumn, 1989 definitely were among the first significant signs of this shift in climate. As stated earlier, the opening of the borders and the resignation of Egon Krenz's old government mark the ideological collapse of the old regime. The interim phase (November 1989 to March 1990) was, for many GDR citizens, a very exciting but frighteningly chaotic time. From December 7, 1989, the GDR was increasingly governed by two powers. Besides (or rather, in opposition to) the Modrow government, the 'Round Table' – a forum of citizen movements, churches, and various political parties (some newly founded) – became a political force, developing alternative plans for the political, economic, and educational development of the GDR. Specific changes introduced into the education system will be examined later in this chapter.

On January 15, 1990, Hans Modrow, head of a GDR government still dominated by old party members, offered the 'Round Table' participation in the political decision-making process at the highest level of government. The result was the formation, a few weeks later, of the 'Government of National Responsibility'. However, the GDR's first free elections (March 18, 1990) not only led to a definitive loss of power for the Communists, but also pushed the citizens' movements (which had played such an important role in the weakening of the authoritarian state as well as in the interim phase of educational transition) on a 'route to oblivion' (Dahrendorf, 1991, p. 94).

The following months were dedicated to preparations for the reunification of Germany. New legislation was passed, almost on a continuous basis, to pave the way. A treaty between the GDR and the FRG (which included provision for introduction of a common currency) made possible the economic and social union of the two states on July 1, 1990. A second state treaty, the *Einigungsvertrag*, laid down the conditions of unification (i.e. the end of the GDR as a separate political

---

1   However, the group of Oxford researchers has been aware of the limitations of diagrams, which suggest a stone dropped into the water, as in Figure 7. For example, one could argue that the lines of the waves caused by a stone normally do not match the assumptions of *directionality* that one finds in complex political, economic, and social processes.

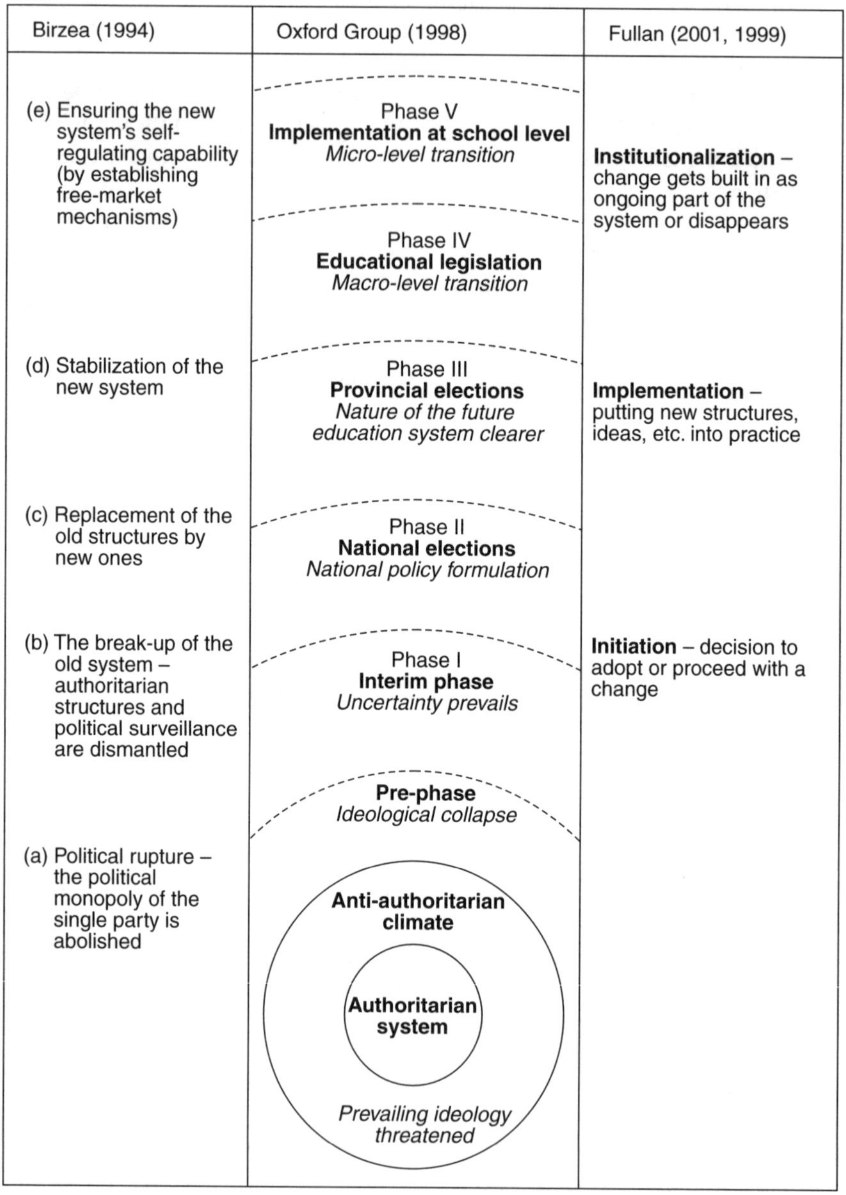

Birzea (1994)	Oxford Group (1998)	Fullan (2001, 1999)
(e) Ensuring the new system's self-regulating capability (by establishing free-market mechanisms)	Phase V **Implementation at school level** *Micro-level transition*	**Institutionalization** – change gets built in as ongoing part of the system or disappears
	Phase IV **Educational legislation** *Macro-level transition*	
(d) Stabilization of the new system	Phase III **Provincial elections** *Nature of the future education system clearer*	**Implementation** – putting new structures, ideas, etc. into practice
(c) Replacement of the old structures by new ones	Phase II **National elections** *National policy formulation*	
(b) The break-up of the old system – authoritarian structures and political surveillance are dismantled	Phase I **Interim phase** *Uncertainty prevails*	**Initiation** – decision to adopt or proceed with a change
	Pre-phase *Ideological collapse*	
(a) Political rupture – the political monopoly of the single party is abolished	**Anti-authoritarian climate** / **Authoritarian system** / *Prevailing ideology threatened*	

Figure 7 The process of educational transition – a comparison of three conceptual models.

entity as of October 3).[2] Once the federal structure had been reintroduced in the East, subsequent provincial elections led to more certainties in the school system, as education in Germany is mainly the responsibility of the states (*Länder*).

The three models or schemas shown in Figure 7[3] were developed for different purposes. Whereas the models devised by Bîrzea and by the Oxford Group[4] attempt to cover both political transition in general and transformation of education systems in particular, Fullan's model was originally developed for understanding educational change within the North American context. However, as the diagram shows, Fullan's model may provide a metaconcept allowing the division of transition processes, on the macro- as well as on the micro-level, into three major phases. This approach is supported by Fullan's remark (referring to Anderson's notion of 'multiple innovations') that 'when we identify factors affecting successful initiation and implementation, [we] should think of these factors as operating across many innovations – and many levels of the system (classroom, school, district, state, nation)' (Fullan, 2001, p. 52).

Examination of the transformation of the East German education system reveals the important fact that new educational structures or plans were sometimes discontinued even after successful implementation. There may be a variety of reasons for this phenomenon. After the 1989 collapse of the Communist state, a variety of initiatives were introduced, many of which directly addressed the old system's shortcomings. Traditional instruction methods, which were perceived as too teacher-centred and often dull and monotonous, were replaced by a more child-centred approach; concepts inspired by the reform pedagogy of the beginning of the century (e.g. interdisciplinary studies and project learning) began to emerge. However, not all of the innovations corresponded to the new demands of the unified republic;[5] as a result, some of these trends disappeared or diminished

2   The GDR joined the FRG under Article 23 of the Basic Law of the Federal Republic of Germany.
3   I have attempted to arrange the stages of transition or change as identified by Bîrzea (1994), the Oxford Group (McLeish and Phillips, 1998), and Fullan (2001) in such a way as to allow comparison of the three approaches.
4   McLeish, who describes the model of the Oxford Group in detail (McLeish, 1998, pp. 15–21), stresses that by the time of the 'pre-phase', the finite boundary of the authoritarian system has been replaced by one which not only is far more vague in its general shape, but also lacks any means of keeping out 'alien' influences and of preserving the integrity of the prevailing ideology (p. 16). Phase I is characterized by uncertainty about the future political and economic system. This phase is delimited by national and provincial elections, i.e. by Phases II and III. During these phases, the future nature of the education system becomes clearer. However, McLeish (1998, p. 18) also points to the subdivision of the process into two parts: the macro- and the micro-level transition. Whereas the former has to do with changes in structure and legislation, the latter involves the far more complex 'inner' transitions of institutions and individuals.
5   One of the reasons is identified by Wilde (1998, p. 83): 'The concept of *Leistung* (achievement; other terms include *Leistungsdruck*, the pressure to achieve) is highly important within German society in general and the education system in particular. There was a great deal of pressure on East Germany to be able to respond to the new demands placed upon it by its western counterpart, namely for *Leistung* in the education system.'

in the 1990s. In fact, certain GDR experiences and methods which had originally been strongly rejected were revisited by the decade's end.[6]

Change can be described in different ways, with models of educational transition focusing either on macro- or on micro-level change. As we shall see, the kinds of development which correspond to the respective levels of change have different features. What follows is a detailed examination of educational transition in East Germany which explores the various features of change in different education subsystems.

Changes in the school system

For many involved in the initiation of educational change in East Germany, the first few months after the collapse of the communist system seemed a time when 'everything is possible' (Bîrzea, 1994, p. 16). Obedience to aspects of the old rule and eagerness for new approaches led a strange coexistence. Teachers and schools (often under pressure from parents) took the initiative in abolishing school subjects, such as the notorious civic instruction, which were most strongly linked to the communist ideology; at the same time, student-teachers in institutions of higher learning were still being trained to teach the subject. Arnhold (1998, p. 65) describes the amazing acceleration of events during this interim phase. On October 1, 1989, the most influential citizens' movement, 'Neues Forum',[7] presented a list of pressing problems. Among their demands was 'a change in the principles of admission and selection in education, science, and culture'. Their call for the 'awakening of the People's Education and the step away from discipline and boredom' mirrors the climate of that time: the GDR was perceived as still asleep, haunted by shadows of the 'double nightmare of Stalinism and Brezhnevism' (Dahrendorf, 1991, p. 38).

In November 1989, in the space of a few days, the government introduced major changes to the education system in response to the demonstrators' demands. Upon the forced resignation of Minister of Education Margot Honecker (the wife of state and party leader Erich Honecker), military lessons were abolished. A few days later, the government declared that Russian language studies would no longer be compulsory in GDR schools; neither would membership in the Free German Youth (the Communist youth organization). Also addressed during this period was a structural shortcoming of the ten-grade Polytechnical School,[8] which, although designed for all GDR pupils seven to sixteen years of age, allowed for very little differentiation in terms of student needs, interests, or skill levels. The government's introduction in February 1990 of specialized

6　For example, Saxony considered reintroducing the so-called 'Kopfnoten', i.e. marks for discipline, order, participation, and diligence.

7　Legislation recognizing this group was one of the first demands at the autumn demonstrations.

8　This refers to the general ten-grade school for all pupils.

courses – the so-called achievement classes – for a variety of subjects could also be perceived as a reaction to reform-movement criticism.

Weiler *et al.* (1996) have characterized this first phase of the transition process in the GDR as a time of 'grass-roots upheaval'. In the power vacuum that followed the collapse of the old authoritarian structures, some teachers started to experiment with new methods; others were simply relieved to have the ideological burden removed from their shoulders; still others were afraid of things to come, and adhered to the practices they had always followed in the classroom. This period of experimentation came to an end in 1990–91 with the introduction of ready-made solutions: teaching methods, course content, and teaching materials provided by the West. Weiler *et al.* (1996, p. 65), who conducted interviews with teachers in East Germany, further describes this:

> There is a small group of educators in each state that … are or had been active participants in the recent reform … They tell of hopes, stimulation, and activity during the transition period 1989–90 when educational policy was made at the local level and schools were left to chart their own course. 'We wanted to create something of our own,' finds broad consent among these educators.

Education in Germany falls mainly under the authority of the individual states; the states' different approaches are harmonized to some extent by the Standing Conference of the Ministers of Culture. Guiding principles for the school systems were laid down in the Hamburg Agreement of 1964. Prior to German Unification in 1990, all GDR pupils attended a single type of institution, the ten-grade Polytechnical School;[9] however, the school system of the FRG is divided horizontally (and, at the secondary level, also vertically). After primary school (four to six grades), FRG students are streamed into three types of schools: the *Hauptschule* (up to grade nine or ten), the *Realschule* (up to grade ten), and the *Gymnasium* (up to grade thirteen). Over the last decades, the prestigious, academically oriented *Gymnasium* has substantially opened to a broader student population. The *Hauptschule* has been described as the 'school for leftovers', and is generally perceived as the 'problem child' of the German school system.[10]

The tripartite system of secondary education was adopted by the East German states with some modifications. These modifications were linked to the problematic status of the *Hauptschule*. With the exception of Mecklenburg-Western Pomerania,[11]

---

9 The Extended Upper Secondary School (grades eleven to twelve) and some integrated courses (Abitur plus Vocational Training) prepared a small percentage of students (less than 20 per cent of an age cohort) for the Abitur, which served as a prerequisite for admission to institutions of higher education.

10 For more details see Führ (1997).

11 There are five East German states: Saxony, Saxony-Anhalt, Thuringia, Mecklenburg-Western Pomerania, and Brandenburg.

the eastern states were reluctant to establish the *Hauptschule* as a separate type of school. Instead, Saxony, Saxony-Anhalt, and Thuringia established a type of middle school which either included both *Hauptschul* and *Realschul* tracks or offered courses leading to the 'leaving (final) examinations' of both types of school. Only Brandenburg (under the Social Democrats) introduced a comprehensive type of secondary school on a larger scale, i.e. one type of secondary school for the majority of students.[12] The school systems in the eastern states were modelled after those in the West German partner states.[13]

How did GDR teachers cope with these changes? Overnight, they found themselves confronted with a totally unfamiliar education system: Polytechnical Schools were turned into *Hauptschulen,* and Extended Upper-Secondary Schools into *Gymnasia.* Teachers applied for their preferred type of school; however, there was a widespread lack of information (see Wilde, 1998) and, often, the chosen school type was simply the one into which their own institution already had been transformed. About 10 per cent of teachers were dismissed (Weiler *et al.,* 1996). In-service training was provided on a large scale. Change was not limited to types of schools; teachers had to come to terms with new course content (especially in subjects such as history which had been heavily overlaid with communist ideology), new teaching methods (which moved away from 'frontal teaching'), and a variety of new textbooks and other instructional materials. Before 1989, teachers – backed by state authority – were in a strong position to influence parents; under these new conditions, parents had a stronger say in their children's education.

These new features were welcomed by some teachers and looked upon with suspicion by others. For example, many teachers viewed their newly won freedom in the selection and use of teaching materials as an advantage; nevertheless, some persisted for a while in using old GDR textbooks, perceiving them as more systematic (see also Weiler *et al.,* 1996, p. 47). What is more, many teachers suffered from psychological stress as a result of the confusion of changes imposed on them (Phillips, 1995 [1992]). In the months and years following unification, the portrayal of GDR teachers in the media and in public discussions was particularly negative. Rust and Rust (1995, p. 92) offer one explanation for this new phenomenon:

> ... East German teachers had a reputation for being more committed to the ideals of socialism than the broader East German population, mainly because their role was defined by law as being responsible for preparing young people for life in socialism.

12 For more details concerning the school system in the five 'new' states, see Führ (1995 [1992]). Wilde (1998) provides an account of the role of the comprehensive school in Brandenburg.
13 These partnerships were established after 1989 and led to massive support from the West in the form of know-how and human resources.

In the early 1990s, teachers perceived themselves as scapegoats, blamed for negative aspects of the GDR education system (Weiler *et al.*, 1996). Recently, however, there has been a growing tendency among teachers, as in society at large, to discuss more freely the advantages and shortcomings of both systems (Streitwieser, 2000).

The transformation of higher education and research

According to Bieber (1994), the main differences between the higher education systems in the GDR and FRG can be summarized as follows.

- GDR higher education institutions were smaller and had fewer students than those of West Germany.
- Fewer students of an age cohort studied in higher education institutions in the East (13 per cent) than in the West (25 per cent).
- In the GDR, the choice of courses of study was strictly regulated according to the needs of the economy.
- East German higher education institutions had significantly greater numbers of employees than those of West Germany. Although these East German institutions had rather few professorships, they maintained a sizable permanent middle-level academic teaching force.[14] In West Germany, such teaching positions were normally of limited duration and individuals typically accepted them in order to further their academic qualifications.
- In the East, programme organization resembled that of secondary schools, with Marxism-Leninism, Russian, and sports occupying 20 per cent of the timetable. Students received scholarships, the largest part of which went toward accommodation in student residences. Bieber (1994) notes that because of the internal efficiency of the Eastern school system, graduation rates were substantially higher in the East than in the West.

In the GDR, some research was carried out at higher education institutions, but for the most part it was concentrated at the Academies – massive research institutions located mainly in Berlin. The Academies did not fit into the research landscape of the united Germany: in the West, non-university research institutions are mainly concerned with applied research; in the GDR, by contrast, the Academies served as centralized research institutions, carrying out the same types of research (i.e. both basic and applied) as the higher education institutions. Once higher education became a state (rather than a federal) responsibility in 1990, an institutional solution was sought for this problem.

---

14 Such academics engaged in teaching are not professors; rather, their status is perhaps comparable to those of research assistants in North American universities.

An important role in the necessary restructuring was played by the Science Council, an advisory body that helps coordinate the higher-education and research policies of the states with those of the federal government (see Arnhold, 1998). In 1990, the Council had laid down 12 main principles for the transformation of East German higher education and research; these included the integration of the specialized higher education institutions into larger units (e.g. universities), the de-specialization of programmes,[15] and the promotion of young scientists. The Science Council evaluated the GDR's Academy institutes and made recommendations regarding the future of higher education institutions. Some of the Academy institutes were allocated to research societies (e.g. the Max Planck Society); others were closed on the basis of negative evaluation reports. The Council also advised the states on whether to maintain or restructure course content at their higher education institutions.

At the outset of the transformation process, unification was seen not merely as a matter of adjusting the East German education system but as an opportunity to discuss the shortcomings of the West German model. Yet, despite the early intentions of those involved in the process, the key word to the restructuring of higher education in the East was 'adjustment'. Although the Science Council opted to allow certain institutions to continue for a moderate-length term[16] (as in the case of some Pedagogical Colleges), the higher institutions were suspended because they did not fit into the new landscape. This policy of adjustment has been the target of much criticism (e.g. Mayntz, 1994), as the West German model of higher education has been and continues to be in serious crisis, partly as a result of its not yet having found an answer to the pressing problem of fast growing student populations.

Following the restructuring of higher education institutions, East German academics had to reapply for their posts – or, to be more precise, to apply for the newly created jobs in a revised system. They were subject to a twofold evaluation: professional ability and 'personal suitability'. Academics whose history included high-level Communist-Party involvement or who had been state-security informants were disqualified. Although deemed necessary, the instatement of this criterion inadvertently led to serious problems. In the former GDR, publication privileges and the right to attend conferences were awarded on the basis not solely of professional merit but also of loyalty to state and party. Thus a side effect of the new evaluation protocol was that it put competing Western researchers, who had not been subjected to the same pressures as their East German colleagues, in a privileged position; the great majority of East German researchers, either for professional or for political reasons, were found 'unsuitable'. Consequently, Western academics were appointed to many positions in

---

15 The GDR programmes focused very much on preparation for a certain profession. There was very little, if any, freedom to choose and combine different courses of study.

16 Although unspecified, the term is probably five to ten years in length.

the East German higher education and research institutions. Moreover, there is a marked difference between subject areas taught by East and West German academics: a higher percentage of East German professors teach the more 'neutral' subjects, such as the natural sciences and mathematics; few East German professors survived the restructuring in less neutral subject areas such as the humanities and education.[17] The middle level academic teaching force was drastically reduced and significantly reorganized to achieve consistency with universities in the West; this put an end to the favourable teacher-student ratio which had prevailed in the East.

The role of West German advisors at all levels of the education system during the transition period cannot be overemphasized. Every step in the creation of the governments of the Eastern states relied on their input. The West provided the textbooks, the structures, and most of the teaching personnel for Eastern institutions; in the 1990–91 academic year, course outlines for higher education were simply copied from institutions in the West. Among Western professors involved in the restructuring process were those motivated by altruism, who provided helpful advice to their Eastern colleagues; others, however, were more interested in the opportunity to further their own careers (see Phillips, 1995 [1992], p. 250).

Conclusions

The process of restructuring of the East German higher education system has been likened to 'cloning' (Weiler *et al.*, 1996). The term is quite apt in describing what happened in other education subsystems as well. In East Germany, as compared to other countries of the former Soviet Bloc, the transition towards democracy catalyzed by German unification, has taken place at a remarkably accelerated rate. However, such acceleration characterizes mainly the political transition; to a lesser extent, the economic (in the East, wages are still lower, the unemployment rate is 16 per cent, and dependency on Western support will most likely continue); and, to a far lesser extent, the cultural. In 1989, after many years of silence and subordination, East Germany awoke to a short spring of activity, experimentation, openness, and a questioning of its past and future; however, unexpectedly, the modus of unification eventuated in a relapse into old behaviour patterns.

On the basis of extensive interviews, Streitwieser (2000) has identified two strategies by which East German teachers have coped with the new situation. One group, discouraged by students' loss of motivation, deeply regrets the reduction

---

17 See also Arnhold *et al.* (1998, p. 5): 'In the territory of the former German Democratic Republic following Unification, processes of "evaluation" of the teaching force have led to widespread dismissal or nonrenewal of contracts, with the consequential charges of unfair treatment that such processes provoke.'

of teachers' responsibility and authority. The other group works together with students to explore how they can best combine elements from the past with the greater creative possibilities available to them today (Streitwieser, 2000, p. 11). It is this latter group of educators with whom real reform can be built.

During unification, the FRG's education system, with its many problematic features, was extended to the East. However, exporting the West German model might even have led to an entrenchment of the problematic aspects of the system. At the same time, arguments against a thorough reform of the higher education system included lack of money, the necessity of acting quickly, and the absence of well-developed alternatives. A comprehensive reform of German higher education is still anticipated.

In the first paragraph of this chapter, we referred to three conceptual frameworks for understanding transition. All three may be applied to educational change in the former German Democratic Republic; each has utility in explaining different aspects of the process. The models developed by the Oxford Group and by Bîrzea focus mainly on macro-level transition (i.e. on the political framework for institutional change). These models may be supplemented by an approach that focuses on the process of change at individual institutions. Fullan's three-phase model of change is valuable both in the conceptualization of transition on the macro-level and in the investigation of change at individual institutions.

References

Arnhold, N., Bekker, J., Kersh, N., McLeish, E. and Phillips, D. (Eds) (1998) *Education for Reconstruction: The Regeneration of Educational Capacity Following National Upheaval* (Series: *Oxford Studies in Comparative Education*). Wallingford, Oxfordshire: Triangle Books.

Arnhold, N. (1998) The transformation of East German teacher education. In E. A. McLeish and D. Phillips (Eds), *Processes of Transition in Education Systems* (Series: *Oxford Studies in Comparative Education*) (pp. 61–74). Wallingford, Oxfordshire: Triangle Books.

Bieber, H. J. (1994) Die Empfehlungen des Wissenschaftsrates für die Hochschulen in den neuen Ländern [The recommendations of the Science Council for the Higher Education Institutions in the New Federal States]. *Das Hochschulwesen*, 2, 62–71.

Bîrzea, C. (1994) *Educational Policies of the Countries in Transition*. Strasbourg: Council of Europe Press.

Bîrzea, C. (1996) Education in a world in transition: between post-communism and post-modernism. *Prospects*, 100, 673–681.

Dahrendorf, R. (1991) *Reflections on the Revolution in Europe: In a letter intended to have been sent to a gentleman in Warsaw*. London: Chatto & Windus.

Führ, C. (1995) On the education system of the five new *Länder* of the Federal Republic of Germany. In D. Phillips (Ed.), *Education in Germany: Tradition and Reform in Historical Context* (pp. 259–281). London & New York: Routledge.

Führ, C. (1997) *The German Education System Since 1945: Outlines and Problems*. Bonn: Inter Nationes.

Fullan, M. (2001) *The New Meaning of Educational Change* (3rd edn). New York: Teachers College Press.

Mayntz, R. (Ed.) (1994) *Aufbruch und Reform von oben: Ostdeutsche Universitäten im Transformationsprozeß* [*Awakening and Reform from Above: East German Universities in the Transition Process*]. Frankfurt a. M. *et al.*: Campus.

McLeish, E. A. and Phillips, D. (Eds) (1998) *Processes of Transition in Education Systems* (Series: *Oxford Studies in Comparative Education*). Wallingford, Oxfordshire: Triangle Books.

O'Donnell, G. and Schmitter, P. (1986) *Transition from Authoritarian Rule*. Baltimore: John Hopkins University Press.

Phillips, D. (1995 [1992]) Transitions and traditions: Educational developments in the New Germany in their historical context. In D. Phillips (Ed.), *Education in Germany: Tradition and Reform in Historical Context* (International Development in School Reform) (pp. 243–258). London & New York: Routledge.

Rust, V. D. and Rust, D. (1995) *The Unification of German Education*. New York & London: Garland Publishing.

Streitwieser, B. T. (2000, March) Negotiating transformation: East Berlin teachers at the end of the post-unification decade. Paper presented at the annual CIES Conference, San Antonio, Texas, USA.

Weiler, H. N., Mintrop, H. A. and Fuhrmann, E. (1996) *Educational Change and Social Transformation: Teachers, Schools and Universities in Eastern Germany* (Stanford Series on Education & Public Policy). London: The Falmer Press.

Wilde, S. (1998) Reforming or conforming? The case of the Gesamtschule in post-1989 educational reform in Eastern Germany. In E. A. McLeish and D. Phillips (Ed.), *Processes of Transition in Education Systems* (Series: *Oxford Studies in Comparative Education*) (pp. 75–99). Wallingford, Oxfordshire: Triangle Books.

Part III

CROSS-CASE REFLECTIONS

7

THE EMERGENCE OF A CONCEPTUAL FRAMEWORK

Michael Fullan
Ontario Institute for Studies in Education
University of Toronto

In Chapter 1, I introduced the Triple I model – initiation, implementation, institutionalization – as a framework for understanding and guiding educational reform. I supplemented this model with three additional factors which I suggested must be taken into account with respect to large-scale reform: the problem of multiple innovations or 'coherence-making'; the balance between pressure (accountability) and support (capacity-building); and the building of new infrastructures to support reform on a continuous basis.

The Triple I model was applied to each of the five case studies in Part II. I briefly review these applications and conclude by suggesting additional factors arising from each case. In the first case study, Polyzoi and Dneprov examine the transformation of Russia since 1991. In particular, they find that the eight factors identified as features of the initiation phase (see Chapter 1) help explain the strengths and weaknesses of the Russian strategy. They conclude that the Russian transformation freed up possibilities for reform, but that there was insufficient 'understanding' to support new methods and approaches. In other words, the new regime permitted and encouraged decentralization, but local capacity was not sufficiently developed to take advantage of the new opportunities. In terms of the Triple I model, one could conclude that although a long period (a decade) of initiation has been in play, insufficient attention has been paid to implementation capacities. The latter should now be the priority; this includes local capacity as well as capacity at the level of the infrastructure (e.g. teacher preparation, leadership development, curricular material and practices, monitoring devices, and the like).

Polyzoi and Černá's case study of the Czech Republic represents a valuable complement to the Russian study because it focuses on implementation. After 40 years of Communist rule, the Czech Republic moved more rapidly than Russia to dismantle old structures and to proceed through initiation toward implementation. Polyzoi and Černá utilize the three sets of implementation factors (i.e. the specific nature of the reform, local characteristics, and external factors) as a framework for analysis of the Czech case.

Polyzoi and Černá find that, for the most part, the model helps explain implementation or the lack thereof. They suggest that a better understanding of the dynamics of societal transformation may be achieved by supplementing the Triple I model with four principles formulated by Venda:

Principle 1   Systems in transition are typically characterized by the coexistence of old and new structures.
Principle 2   The emergent new 'state' may have few common elements with the 'old', and the wider apart the two states are initially (i.e. when there are no or few overlapping elements), the more difficult the transition process.
Principle 3   If, as the old state begins to transform, its initial drop in efficiency is too steep, the system may enter a chaotic state and collapse.
Principle 4   The transformation process is not unidimensional but affected by multiple factors simultaneously.

The two models together enable the authors to analyse the Czech case.

The third case study in Part II – Hungary – further adds to the knowledge base for understanding transformation. The Triple I model is again effective, but only to a point. Hungary represents a more complete case of reform across the three stages of initiation, implementation and institutionalization. The study also provides a more specific focus on the details of implementation. Halász lists some of the outcomes of reform:

• Schools have become more open to community involvement.
• Cross-disciplinary curriculum approaches are more evident.
• A focus on special needs students has expanded.
• There is a dramatic increase in the need for in-service training of teachers and principals.
• The traditional relationship between staff and principal has been radically altered.
• The sense of professional responsibility among principals and teachers has increased.

Again, Halász supplements the Triple I model with the following conclusions about societies in transition:

1   Educational changes are strongly related to processes outside the education sector.
2   The change process is not a linear one.
3   The capacity to manage uncertainty is a critical factor.
4   Greater willingness to take risks is endemic to societies in transition.
5   Communication and ongoing learning become particularly important.
6   Efficiency in the use of resources increases with experience.
7   A pragmatic approach focusing on the instruments of implementation predominates over abstract theoretical conceptions of change.

The Romanian case study by Bîrzea shows what happens when major structural reforms occur without concomitant changes in the capacity of the infrastructure. Major structural reforms funded through foreign aid were put in place in the 1993–1996 period. These changes were aimed at democratization of the educational system and improved quality of education. A new legislative framework was introduced which specified goals and objectives of education, new managerial structures, curricula, textbooks, evaluation tools, and teacher training.

Once again we see evidence that structural changes are not sufficient and that change in capacity (or what we have called 'reculturing') is a more long-term process. In the third International Mathematics and Science Survey, Romania ranked 34th in mathematics out of 41 participating countries, and 31st in sciences. The Czech Republic finished 2nd in sciences and 6th in mathematics; Hungary ranked 9th and 14th. As Bîrzea points out, education reform is more advanced than economic reform in Romania; consequently, internal resources are not yet sufficiently developed for implementation of the reforms. He calls for improvement in key national institutions (inspectorates, teacher staff centres, universities), in local school and community development, and in the nature and quality of teacher education.

Arnhold examines the East German education system as it was transformed (i.e. 'absorbed') by the Federal Republic of Germany (FRG) following the collapse of the Berlin Wall, and the signing of the Unification Treaty. The experience of East Germany, in moving from a planned market economy and authoritarian control towards democracy, was remarkably accelerated in its early stages – with a strange co-existence of the old and the new systems. However, in the course of unification, some of the more problematic features of the FRG education system were also extended to the East, resulting in a gradual, more cautious approach to change, and even some retrenchment. A comprehensive reform of German higher education is still anticipated.

Conclusions

The ideas that emerge from these case studies together with recent conceptual developments in complexity theory provide a broad framework for understanding the transformation of education in contexts of societal change – one which may help guide our thinking and strategic planning. Specifically, the combination of Venda's four principles of transition, the Triple I model, and Wallace and Pocklington's (in press) four-change management themes, results in a more dynamic model better suited to helping us understand societal transformation. Venda's four principles of transition form the underlying assumptions of the Triple I/Change theme matrix of Table 1.

Table 1 represents the broad components of a potential framework. In the meantime, further case studies which seek to characterize the dynamic process of change across time – by identifying critical factors and themes, their consequences and impact – will provide further insights into societies undergoing transition.

Table 1 A conceptual framework for educational transformation.

Assumptions:

1 Systems in transition are characterized by the coexistence of old and new structures.
2 The emergent new 'state' may have few common elements with the 'old', and the greater the discrepancy, the more difficult the transition.
3 If the initial drop in efficiency of the old state is too steep, the system may enter a chaotic state.
4 The transformation process is affected by multiple factors simultaneously.

Change management themes

	Metatask of orchestration	Flexible planning and coordination	Culture building and communication	Differentiated support
Initiation Implementation Institutionalization	Establishing multiple communication links across the three stages; establishing and developing structures to support change	Coordinating/planning across all levels	Articulating a vision and developing it in practice across all stakeholders	Establishing pressure and support strategies for developing capacity and monitoring results

The case studies in this book make a significant contribution to this growing knowledge base which will be essential for understanding, as well as for guiding, educational reform in societies undergoing major transformation.

Wallace and Pocklington (in press) used complexity theory to examine large-scale reform in England. In particular they identified four tasks – orchestration, flexible planning, culture building, and differential support. These tasks align with the three stages of the Triple I model. Finally, the four basic assumptions underpin the evolution of reform across time.

System transformation is enormously complex, and cannot be blueprinted in advance. What is needed is a broad new vision, a statement of directional goals, and mechanisms (strategies and structures) for implementation, monitoring and problem-solving as the reform evolves. It is a matter of maintaining a strong press for reform, realizing that the process will be anxiety-producing, and having the structures in place so that the tensions do not become overwhelming, i.e. chaotic (see Fullan, 2003).

As to who oversees the four change management themes, it is necessary that a system be developed consisting of a Steering Group or comparable body, and a set of authority roles and responsibilities for working through implementation attending to (1) two-way communication (downward and upward); (2) planning across school/regional and state levels; (3) capacities required for implementation in practice; and (4) monitoring results in a problem-solving mode which feeds back into the three previous processes.

The advice is that reformers should design strategies using these guidelines, and that corresponding case studies document and analyse the nature and impact of the strategies.

In conclusion, let me suggest that successful educational reform is a function of the fusion of three powerful forces – the intellectual, the political, and the spiritual or moral (Fullan, 1999). In other words, we need quality ideas, power, and purpose.

We do not often think of teachers as being in the business of scientific breakthroughs. Yet it is increasingly clear in the knowledge society that continuous knowledge development and sharing is crucial for solving problems. Thus, any strategy of reform must establish processes for generating and accessing knowledge and best practices.

The second dimension is mobilizing power to get things done. Except in extreme cases this does not mean overpowering the opposition. For implementation to be successful, power means focusing on reconciling differences and establishing alliances among diverse parties. You cannot alter a complex system unless you mobilize a critical mass of different groups working together.

Moral purpose or the spiritual dimension of education reform involves elevating the debate and commitment of large numbers of people to make a difference in the lives of students. Moreover, in system transformation this takes on a much larger role because it involves raising the bar and closing the gap of high and low performers and helping to improve society as a whole through the development of the capacity of future citizens. I have argued elsewhere that this means that educators at all levels must learn to connect to the 'bigger picture' (Fullan, 2003).

Now that the initial upheaval of the transformation of countries has been experienced, the next stage should involve more informal, in-depth strategies for implementing and sustaining large-scale reform. We are now in a position to use what we know to obtain greater success, and to learn from these new attempts how to go even deeper.

References

Fullan, M. (1999) *Change Forces: The Sequel*. London: Falmer Press.

Fullan, M. (2003) *Change Forces with a Vengeance*. London: Routledge-Falmer Press.

Wallace, M. and Pocklington, K. (2002) *Managing Complex Educational Change: Large-Scale Reorganisation of Schools*. London: Routledge.

INDEX